CEOE
Field 25

OSAT
Middle Level-
Intermediate
Mathematics
Teacher Certification Exam

By: Sharon Wynne, M.S.
Southern Connecticut State University

"And, while there's no reason yet to panic, I think it's only prudent that we make preparations to panic."

XAMonline, INC.
Boston

XAMonline, Inc.
21 Orient Ave.
Melrose, MA 02176
Toll Free 1-800-509-4128
Email: info@xamonline.com
Web www.xamonline.com
Fax: 1-781-662-9268

Library of Congress Cataloging-in-Publication Data

Wynne, Sharon A.
    OSAT Middle Level-Intermediate Mathematics Field 25: Teacher Certification / Sharon A. Wynne. -2nd ed. ISBN 978-1-58197-647-2
    1. OSAT Middle Level-Intermediate Mathematics Field 25.   2. Study Guides.
    3. CEOE   4. Teachers' Certification & Licensure.   5. Careers

Disclaimer:

The opinions expressed in this publication are the sole works of XAMonline and were created independently from the National Education Association, Educational Testing Service, or any State Department of Education, National Evaluation Systems or other testing affiliates.

Between the time of publication and printing, state specific standards as well as testing formats and website information may change that is not included in part or in whole within this product. Sample test questions are developed by XAMonline and reflect similar content as on real tests; however, they are not former tests. XAMonline assembles content that aligns with state standards but makes no claims nor guarantees teacher candidates a passing score. Numerical scores are determined by testing companies such as NES or ETS and then are compared with individual state standards. A passing score varies from state to state.

Printed in the United States of America   œ-1

CEOE: OSAT Middle Level-Intermediate Mathematics Field 25
ISBN: 978-1-58197-647-2

About the Subject Assessments

CEOE™: Subject Assessment in the Middle Level-Intermediate Mathematics examination

Purpose: The assessments are designed to test the knowledge and competencies of prospective secondary level teachers. The question bank from which the assessment is drawn is undergoing constant revision. As a result, your test may include questions that will not count towards your score.

Test Version: There are two versions of subject assessment for Mathematics in Oklahoma. The Middle Level-Intermediate Mathematics (115) exam emphasizes comprehension in Mathematical Processes and Number Sense; Relations, Functions, and Algebra; Measurement and Geometry; Probability, Statistics, and Discrete Mathematics. The Advanced Mathematics (011) exam emphasizes comprehension in Mathematical Processes and Number Sense; Relations, Functions, and Algebra; Measurement and Geometry; Probability, Statistics, and Discrete Mathematics. The Middle Level-Intermediate Mathematics study guide is based on a typical knowledge level of persons who have completed a *bachelor's degree program* in Mathematics.

Time Allowance, Format and Scoring: You will have 4 hours to finish the exam. There are approximately 80 multiple-choice questions and one constructed-response question in the exam. 85% of your total score consists of selected-response questions; 15% of your total score consists of the constructed response question

Weighting: There is one constructed-response question in Relation, Functions, and Algebra.

Additional Information about the CEOE Assessments: The CEOE series subject assessments are developed by *National Evaluation Systems.* They provide additional information on the CEOE series assessments, including registration, preparation and testing procedures and study materials such topical guides that have about 28 pages of information including approximately 11 additional sample questions.

Table of Contents

Great Study and Testing Tips!

What to study in order to prepare for the subject assessments is the focus of this study guide but equally important is *how* you study.

You can increase your chances of truly mastering the information by taking some simple, but effective steps.

Study Tips:

1. Some foods aid the learning process. Foods such as milk, nuts, seeds, rice, and oats help your study efforts by releasing natural memory enhancers called CCKs (*cholecystokinin*) composed of *tryptophan*, *choline*, and *phenylalanine*. All of these chemicals enhance the neurotransmitters associated with memory. Before studying, try a light, protein-rich meal of eggs, turkey, and fish. All of these foods release the memory enhancing chemicals. The better the connections, the more you comprehend.

Likewise, before you take a test, stick to a light snack of energy boosting and relaxing foods. A glass of milk, a piece of fruit, or some peanuts all release various memory-boosting chemicals and help you to relax and focus on the subject at hand.

2. Learn to take great notes. A by-product of our modern culture is that we have grown accustomed to getting our information in short doses (i.e. TV news sound bites or USA Today style newspaper articles.)

Consequently, we've subconsciously trained ourselves to assimilate information better in neat little packages. If your notes are scrawled all over the paper, it fragments the flow of the information. Strive for clarity. Newspapers use a standard format to achieve clarity. Your notes can be much clearer through use of proper formatting. A very effective format is called the *"Cornell Method."*

> Take a sheet of loose-leaf lined notebook paper and draw a line all the way down the paper about 1-2" from the left-hand edge.

> Draw another line across the width of the paper about 1-2" up from the bottom. Repeat this process on the reverse side of the page.

Look at the highly effective result. You have ample room for notes, a left hand margin for special emphasis items or inserting supplementary data from the textbook, a large area at the bottom for a brief summary, and a little rectangular space for just about anything you want.

3. <u>Get the concept then the details</u>. Too often we focus on the details and don't gather an understanding of the concept. However, if you simply memorize only dates, places, or names, you may well miss the whole point of the subject.

A key way to understand things is to put them in your own words. If you are working from a textbook, automatically summarize each paragraph in your mind. If you are outlining text, don't simply copy the author's words.

Rephrase them in your own words. You remember your own thoughts and words much better than someone else's, and subconsciously tend to associate the important details to the core concepts.

4. <u>Ask Why?</u> Pull apart written material paragraph by paragraph and don't forget the captions under the illustrations.

Example: If the heading is "Stream Erosion", flip it around to read "Why do streams erode?" Then answer the questions.

If you train your mind to think in a series of questions and answers, not only will you learn more, but it also helps to lessen the test anxiety because you are used to answering questions.

5. <u>Read for reinforcement and future needs</u>. Even if you only have 10 minutes, put your notes or a book in your hand. Your mind is similar to a computer; you have to input data in order to have it processed. *By reading, you are creating the neural connections for future retrieval.* The more times you read something, the more you reinforce the learning of ideas.

Even if you don't fully understand something on the first pass, *your mind stores much of the material for later recall.*

6. <u>Relax to learn so go into exile</u>. Our bodies respond to an inner clock called biorhythms. Burning the midnight oil works well for some people, but not everyone.

If possible, set aside a particular place to study that is free of distractions. Shut off the television, cell phone, pager and exile your friends and family during your study period.

If you really are bothered by silence, try background music. Light classical music at a low volume has been shown to aid in concentration over other types. Music that evokes pleasant emotions without lyrics are highly suggested. Try just about anything by Mozart. It relaxes you.

7. <u>Use arrows not highlighters</u>. At best, it's difficult to read a page full of yellow, pink, blue, and green streaks. Try staring at a neon sign for a while and you'll soon see that the horde of colors obscure the message.

A quick note, a brief dash of color, an underline, and an arrow pointing to a particular passage is much clearer than a horde of highlighted words.

8. <u>Budget your study time</u>. Although you shouldn't ignore any of the material, *allocate your available study time in the same ratio that topics may appear on the test.*

Testing Tips:

1. Get smart, play dumb. Don't read anything into the question. Don't make an assumption that the test writer is looking for something else than what is asked. Stick to the question as written and don't read extra things into it.

2. Read the question and all the choices _twice_ before answering the question. You may miss something by not carefully reading, and then re-reading both the question and the answers.

If you really don't have a clue as to the right answer, leave it blank on the first time through. Go on to the other questions, as they may provide a clue as to how to answer the skipped questions.

If later on, you still can't answer the skipped ones . . . **Guess.** The only penalty for guessing is that you _might_ get it wrong. Only one thing is certain; if you don't put anything down, you will get it wrong!

3. Turn the question into a statement. Look at the way the questions are worded. The syntax of the question usually provides a clue. Does it seem more familiar as a statement rather than as a question? Does it sound strange?

By turning a question into a statement, you may be able to spot if an answer sounds right, and it may also trigger memories of material you have read.

4. Look for hidden clues. It's actually very difficult to compose multiple-foil (choice) questions without giving away part of the answer in the options presented.

In most multiple-choice questions you can often readily eliminate one or two of the potential answers. This leaves you with only two real possibilities and automatically your odds go to Fifty-Fifty for very little work.

5. Trust your instincts. For every fact that you have read, you subconsciously retain something of that knowledge. On questions that you aren't really certain about, go with your basic instincts. **Your first impression on how to answer a question is usually correct.**

6. Mark your answers directly on the test booklet. Don't bother trying to fill in the optical scan sheet on the first pass through the test.

Just be very careful not to miss-mark your answers when you eventually transcribe them to the scan sheet.

7. Watch the clock! You have a set amount of time to answer the questions. Don't get bogged down trying to answer a single question at the expense of 10 questions you can more readily answer.

THIS PAGE BLANK

SUBAREA I.   MATHEMATICAL PROCESSES AND NUMBER SENSE

Competency 0001   **Understand mathematical problem solving and the connections between and among the fields of mathematics and other disciplines.**

Successful math teachers introduce their students to multiple problem solving strategies and create a classroom environment where free thought and experimentation are encouraged. Teachers can promote problem solving by allowing multiple attempts at problems, giving credit for reworking test or homework problems, and encouraging the sharing of ideas through class discussion. There are several specific problem solving skills with which teachers should be familiar.

The **guess-and-check** strategy calls for students to make an initial guess at the solution, check the answer, and use the outcome of to guide the next guess. With each successive guess, the student should get closer to the correct answer. Constructing a table from the guesses can help organize the data.

Example:

There are 100 coins in a jar. 10 are dimes. The rest are pennies and nickels. There are twice as many pennies as nickels. How many pennies and nickels are in the jar?

There are 90 total nickels and pennies in the jar (100 coins – 10 dimes).

There are twice as many pennies as nickels. Make guesses that fulfill the criteria and adjust based on the answer found. Continue until we find the correct answer, 60 pennies and 30 nickels.

Number of Pennies	Number of Nickels	Total Number of Pennies and Nickels
40	20	60
80	40	120
70	35	105
60	30	90

When solving a problem where the final result and the steps to reach the result are given, students must **work backwards** to determine what the starting point must have been.

Example:

John subtracted seven from his age, and divided the result by 3. The final result was 4. What is John's age?

Work backward by reversing the operations.
$4 \times 3 = 12$;
$12 + 7 = 19$
John is 19 years old.

Estimation and testing for **reasonableness** are related skills students should employ both before and after solving a problem. These skills are particularly important when students use calculators to find answers.

Example:

Find the sum of $4387 + 7226 + 5893$.

$4300 + 7200 + 5800 = 17300$	Estimation.
$4387 + 7226 + 5893 = 17506$	Actual sum.

By comparing the estimate to the actual sum, students can determine that their answer is reasonable.

Example – Life Science

Examine an animal population and vegetation density in a biome over time.

Example – Physical Science

Explore motions and forces by calculating speeds based on distance and time traveled and creating a graph to represent the data.

Example – Geography

Explore and illustrate knowledge of earth landforms.

Example – Economics/Finance

Compare car buying with car leasing by graphing comparisons and setting up monthly payment schedules based on available interest rates.

Mathematics dates back before recorded history. Prehistoric cave paintings with geometrical figures and slash counting have been dated prior to 20,000 BC in Africa and France. The major early uses of mathematics were for astronomy, architecture, trading and taxation.

The early history of mathematics is found in Mesopotamia (Sumeria and Babylon), Egypt, Greece and Rome. Noted mathematicians from these times include Euclid, Pythagoras, Apollonius, Ptolemy and Archimedes.

Islamic culture from the 6th through 12th centuries drew from areas ranging from Africa and Spain to India. Through India, they also drew on China. This mix of cultures and ideas brought about developments in many areas, including the concept of algebra, our current numbering system, and major developments in algebra with concepts such as zero. India was the source of many of these developments. Notable scholars of this era include Omar Khayyam and Muhammad al-Khwarizmi.

Counting boards have been found in archeological digs in Babylonia and Greece. These include the Chinese abacus whose current form dates from approximately 1200 AD. Prior to the development of the zero, a counting board or abacus was the common method used for all types of calculations.

Abelard and Fibonacci brought Islamic texts to Europe in the 12th century. By the 17th century, major new works appeared from Galileo and Copernicus (astronomy), Newton and Leibniz (calculus), and Napier and Briggs (logarithms). Other significant mathematicians of this era include René Descartes, Carl Gauss, Pierre de Fermat, Leonhard Euler and Blaise Pascal.

The growth of mathematics since 1800 has been enormous, and has affected nearly every area of life. Some names significant in the history of mathematics since 1800 (and the work they are most known for):

Joseph-Louis Lagrange (theory of functions and of mechanics)
Pierre-Simon Laplace (celestial mechanics, probability theory)
Joseph Fourier (number theory)
Lobachevsky and Bolyai (non-Euclidean geometry)
Charles Babbage (calculating machines, origin of the computer)
Lady Ada Lovelace (first known program)
Florence Nightingale (nursing, statistics of populations)
Bertrand Russell (logic)
James Maxwell (differential calculus and analysis)
John von Neumann (economics, quantum mechanics and game theory)
Alan Turing (theoretical foundations of computer science)
Albert Einstein (theory of relativity)
Gustav Roch (topology)

Competency 0002   Understand the principles and processes of mathematical reasoning.

In a **2 column proof**, the left side of the proof should be the given information, or statements that could be proved by deductive reasoning. The right column of the proof consists of the reasons used to determine that each statement to the left was verifiably true. The right side can identify given information, or state theorems, postulates, definitions or algebraic properties used to prove that particular line of the proof is true.

Assume the opposite of the conclusion. Keep your hypothesis and given information the same. Proceed to develop the steps of the proof, looking for a statement that contradicts your original assumption or some other known fact. This contradiction indicates that the assumption you made at the beginning of the proof was incorrect; therefore, the original conclusion has to be true.

Inductive thinking is the process of finding a pattern from a group of examples. That pattern is the conclusion that this set of examples seemed to indicate. It may be a correct conclusion or it may be an incorrect conclusion because other examples may not follow the predicted pattern.

Deductive thinking is the process of arriving at a conclusion based on other statements that are all known to be true, such as theorems, axiomspostulates, or postulates. Conclusions found by deductive thinking based on true statements will **always** be true.

Examples:

Suppose:
    On Monday Mr. Peterson eats breakfast at McDonalds.
    On Tuesday Mr. Peterson eats breakfast at McDonalds.
    On Wednesday Mr. Peterson eats breakfast at McDonalds.
    On Thursday Mr. Peterson eats breakfast at McDonalds again.

Conclusion: On Friday Mr. Peterson will eat breakfast at
                    McDonalds again.

This is a conclusion based on inductive reasoning. Based on several days observations, you conclude that Mr. Peterson will eat at McDonalds. This may or may not be true, but it is a conclusion arrived at by inductive thinking.

In searching for mathematic counterexamples, one should consider extreme cases near the ends of the domain of an experiment and special cases where an additional property is introduced.

Examples of extreme cases are numbers near zero and obtuse triangles that are nearly flat. An example of a special case for a problem involving rectangles is a square because a square is a rectangle with the additional property of symmetry.

Example:

Identify a counterexample for the following conjectures.

1. If n is an even number, then $n + 1$ is divisible by 3.

$$n = 4$$
$$n + 1 = 4 + 1 = 5$$
5 is not divisible by 3.

2. If n is divisible by 3, then $n^2 - 1$ is divisible by 4.

$$n = 6$$
$$n^2 - 1 = 6^2 - 1 = 35$$
35 is not divisible by 4.

Proofs by mathematical induction.

Proof by induction states that a statement is true for all numbers if the following two statements can be proven:

1. The statement is true for $n = 1$.
2. If the statement is true for $n = k$, then it is also true for $n = k+1$.

In other words, we must show that the statement is true for a particular value and then we can assume it is true for another, larger value (k). Then, if we can show that the number after the assumed value ($k+1$) also satisfies the statement, we can assume, by induction, that the statement is true for all numbers.

The four basic components of induction proofs are: (1) the statement to be proved, (2) the beginning step ("let $n = 1$"), (3) the assumption step ("let $n = k$ and assume the statement is true for k, and (4) the induction step ("let $n = k+1$").

Example:

Prove that the sum all numbers from 1 to n is equal to $\dfrac{(n)(n+1)}{2}$.

Let $n = 1$.   Beginning step.
Then the sum of 1 to 1 is 1.
And $\dfrac{(n)(n+1)}{2} = 1$.

Thus, the statement is true for $n = 1$.   Statement is true in
                                                a particular
                                                instance.

Assumption:

Let $n = k + 1$
    $k = n - 1$

Then $[1 + 2 + \ldots + k] + (k+1) = \dfrac{(k)(k+1)}{2} + (k+1)$

                                                Substitute the
                                                assumption.

$= \dfrac{(k)(k+1)}{2} + \dfrac{2(k+1)}{2}$

                                                Common
                                                denominator.

$= \dfrac{(k)(k+1) + 2(k+1)}{2}$ Add fractions.

$= \dfrac{(k+2)(k+1)}{2}$ Simplify.

$= \dfrac{(k+1)+1)(k+1)}{2}$

                                                Write in terms of
                                                $k+1$.

For n = 4 , k = 3

$= \dfrac{(4+1)(4)}{2} = \dfrac{20}{2} = 10$

Conclude that the original statement is true for $n = k+1$ if it is
assumed that the statement is true for $n = k$.

Proofs on a coordinate plane

Use proofs on the coordinate plane to prove properties of geometric figures. Coordinate proofs often utilize formulas such as the Distance Formula, Midpoint Formula, and the Slope Formula.

The most important step in coordinate proofs is the placement of the figure on the plane. Place the figure in such a way to make the mathematical calculations as simple as possible.

Example:

1. Prove that the square of the length of the hypotenuse of triangle ABC is equal to the sum of the squares of the lengths of the legs using coordinate geometry.

Draw and label the graph.

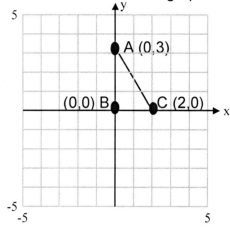

Use the distance formula to find the lengths of the sides of the triangle.

$$d = \sqrt{(x_2 - x_1)^2 + (y_2 - y_1)^2}$$

AB = $\sqrt{3^2} = 3$, BC = $\sqrt{2^2} = 2$, AC = $\sqrt{3^2 + 2^2} = \sqrt{13}$

Conclude

$(AB)^2 + (BC)^2 = 3^2 + 2^2 = 13$
$(AC)^2 = (\sqrt{13})^2 = 13$

Thus, $(AB)^2 + (BC)^2 = (AC)^2$

Competency 0003   Understand and communicate mathematical concepts, symbols, and terminology.

Students of mathematics must be able to recognize and interpret the different representations of arithmetic operations. Diagrams of arithmetic operations can present mathematical data in visual form.

For example, we can use the number line to add and subtract.

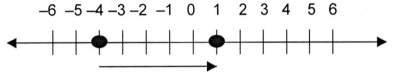

The addition of 5 to -4 on the number line; $-4 + 5 = 1$.

We can also use pictorial representations to explain all of the arithmetic processes.

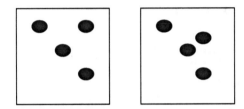

Two groups of four equals eight or $2 \times 4 = 8$ shown in picture form.

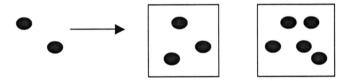

Adding three objects to two or $3 + 2 = 5$ shown in picture form.

The **questioning technique** is a mathematic process skill in which students devise questions to clarify the problem, eliminate possible solutions, and simplify the problem solving process. By developing and attempting to answer simple questions, students can tackle difficult and complex problems.

Observation-inference is a mathematic process skill that is used regularly in statistics. We can use the data gathered or observed from a sample of the population to make inferences about traits and qualities of the population as a whole. For example, if we observe that 40% of voters in our sample favor Candidate A, then we can infer that 40% of the entire voting population favors Candidate A. Successful use of observation-inference depends on accurate observation and representative sampling.

Examples, illustrations, and symbolic representations are useful tools in explaining and understanding mathematical concepts. The ability to create examples and alternative methods of expression allows students to solve real world problems and better communicate their thoughts.

Concrete examples are real world applications of mathematical concepts.

For example, measuring the shadow produced by a tree or building is a real world application of trigonometric functions, acceleration or velocity of a car is an application of derivatives, and finding the volume or area of a swimming pool is a real world application of geometric principles.

Pictorial illustrations of mathematic concepts help clarify difficult ideas and simplify problem solving.

Examples:

1. Rectangle R represents the 300 students in School A. Circle P represents the 150 students that participated in band. Circle Q represents the 170 students that participated in a sport. 70 students participated in both band and a sport.

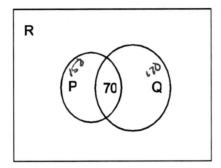

Pictorial representation of above situation.

2. A ball rolls up an incline and rolls back to its original position. Create a graph of the velocity of the ball.

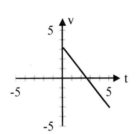

Velocity starts out at its maximum as the ball begins to roll, decreases to zero at the top of the incline, and returns to the maximum in the opposite direction at the bottom of the incline.

Symbolic representation is the basic language of mathematics. Converting data to symbols allows for easy manipulation and problem solving. Students should have the ability to recognize what the symbolic notation represents and convert information into symbolic form. For example, from the graph of a line, students should have the ability to determine the slope and intercepts and derive the line's equation from the observed data.

Another possible application of symbolic representation is the formulation of algebraic expressions and relations from data presented in word problem form.

Competency 0004 **Understand number theory and the principles and properties of the complex number system (i.e., real and imaginary numbers).**

The unit rate for purchasing an item is its price divided by the number of pounds/ounces, etc. in the item. The item with the lower unit rate is the lower price.

Example: Find the item with the best unit price:

$1.79 for 10 ounces
$1.89 for 12 ounces
$5.49 for 32 ounces

$$\frac{1.79}{10} = 0.179 \text{ per ounce} \qquad \frac{1.89}{12} = 0.1575 \text{ per ounce} \qquad \frac{5.49}{32} = 0.172 \text{[SA1] per ounce}$$

$1.89 for 12 ounces is the best price.

A second way to find the better buy is to make a proportion with the price over the number of ounces, etc. Cross multiply the proportion, writing the products above the numerator that is used. The better price will have the smaller product.

Example: Find the better buy:

$8.19 for 40 pounds or $4.89 for 22 pounds

Find the unit price.

$$\frac{40}{8.19} = \frac{1}{x} \qquad\qquad\qquad \frac{22}{4.89} = \frac{1}{x}$$
$$40x = 8.19 \qquad\qquad\qquad 22x = 4.89 \quad \text{[SA2]}$$
$$x = 0.20475 \qquad\qquad\qquad x = 0.22\overline{227}$$

Since $0.20475 < 0.22\overline{227}$ [SA3], $8.19 is less and is a better buy.

To find the amount of sales tax on an item, change the percent of sales tax into an equivalent decimal number. Then multiply the decimal number times the price of the object to find the sales tax. The total cost of an item will be the price of the item plus the sales tax.

Example: A guitar costs $120 plus 7% sales tax. How much are the sales tax and the total bill?

7% = .07 as a decimal   (.07)(120) = $8.40 sales tax
$120 + $8.40 = $128.40 ← total cost

An alternative method to find the total cost is to multiply the price times the factor 1.07 (price + sales tax):

$$\$120 \times 1.07 = \$8.40$$

This gives you the total cost in fewer steps.

[SA4]

Example: A suit costs $450 plus 6½% sales tax. How much are the sales tax and the total bill?

6½% = .065 as a decimal
(.065)(450) = $29.25 sales tax
$450 + $29.25 = $479.25 ← total cost

An alternative method to find the total cost is to multiply the price times the factor 1.065 (price + sales tax):

$$\$450 \times 1.065 = \$479.25$$

This gives you the total cost in fewer steps.

[SA5]

A **ratio** is a comparison of 2 numbers. If a class had 11 boys and 14 girls, the ratio of boys to girls could be written one of 3 ways:

11:14   or   11 to 14   or $\dfrac{11}{14}$

The ratio of girls to boys is:

14:11, 14 to 11 or $\dfrac{14}{11}$

Ratios can be reduced when possible. A ratio of 12 cats to 18 dogs would reduce to 2:3, 2 to 3 or $2/3$.

Note: Read ratio questions carefully. Given a group of 6 adults and 5 children, the ratio of children to the entire group would be 5:11.

A **proportion** is an equation in which a fraction is set equal to another.

To solve the proportion, multiply each numerator times the other fraction's denominator. Set these two products equal to each other and solve the resulting equation. This is called **cross-multiplying** the proportion.

Example: $\dfrac{4}{15} = \dfrac{x}{60}$ is a proportion.

To solve this, cross multiply.

$$(4)(60) = (15)(x)$$
$$240 = 15x$$
$$16 = x$$

Example: $\dfrac{x+3}{3x+4} = \dfrac{2}{5}$ is a proportion.

To solve, cross multiply.

$$5(x + 3) = 2(3x + 4)$$
$$5x + 15 = 6x + 8$$
$$7 = x$$

Example: $\dfrac{x+2}{8} = \dfrac{2}{x-4}$ is another proportion.

To solve, cross multiply.
$$(x+2)(x-4) = 8(2)$$
$$x^2 - 2x - 8 = 16$$
$$x^2 - 2x - 24 = 0$$
$$(x-6)(x+4) = 0$$
$$x = 6 \text{ or } x = {}^-4$$

Both answers work.

Fractions, decimals, and percents can be used interchangeably within problems.

→ To change a percent into a decimal, move the decimal point two places to the left and drop off the percent sign.

→ To change a decimal into a percent, move the decimal two places to the right and add on a percent sign.

→ To change a fraction into a decimal, divide the numerator by the denominator.

→ To change a decimal number into an equivalent fraction, write the decimal part of the number as the fraction's numerator. As the fraction's denominator use the place value of the last column of the decimal. Reduce the resulting fraction as far as possible.

Example: J.C. Nickels has Hunch jeans 1/4 off the usual price of $36.00. Shears and Roadkill have the same jeans 30% off their regular price of $40. Find the cheaper price.

1/4 = .25 so .25(36) = $9.00 off $36 - 9 = $27 sale price

30% = .30 so .30(40) = $12 off $40 - 12 = $28 sale price

The price at J.C Nickels is actually lower.

The **real number properties** are best explained in terms of a small set of numbers. For each property, a given set will be provided.

Axioms of Addition

Closure—For all real numbers a and b, $a + b$ is a unique real number.

Associative—For all real numbers a, b, and c, $(a + b) + c = a + (b + c)$.

Additive Identity—There exists a unique real number 0 (zero) such that $a + 0 = 0 + a = a$ for every real number a.

Additive Inverses—For each real number a, there exists a real number $-a$ (the opposite of a) such that $a + (-a) = (-a) + a = 0$.

Commutative—For all real numbers a and b, $a + b = b + a$.

Axioms of Multiplication

Closure—For all real numbers a and b, ab is a unique real number.

Associative—For all real numbers a, b, and c, $(ab)c = a(bc)$.

Multiplicative Identity—There exists a unique nonzero real number 1 (one) such that $1 \cdot a = a \cdot 1 = a$.

Multiplicative Inverses—For each nonzero rel number, there exists a real number $1/a$ (the reciprocal of a) such that $a(1/a) = (1/a)a = 1$.

Commutative—For all real numbers a and b, $ab = ba$.

The Distributive Axiom of Multiplication over Addition

For all real numbers a, b, and c, $a(b + c) = ab + ac$.

Prime numbers are numbers that can only be factored into 1 and the number itself. When factoring into prime factors, all the factors must be numbers that cannot be factored again (without using 1). Initially numbers can be factored into any 2 factors. Check each resulting factor to see if it can be factored again. Continue factoring until all remaining factors are prime. This is the list of prime factors. Regardless of which way the original number was factored, the final list of prime factors will always be the same.

<u>Example:</u> Factor 30 into prime factors.

Divide by 2 as many times as you can, then by 3, then by other successive primes as required.

$2 \cdot 2 \cdot 2 \cdot 2 \cdot 2 \cdot 2 \cdot 2 \cdot 2 \cdot 2 \cdot 2 \cdot 2 \cdot 2 \cdot 2 \cdot 2 \cdot 2$

[SA6]

Factor 30 into any 2 factors.

$5 \cdot 6$	Now factor the 6.
$5 \cdot 2 \cdot 3$	These are all prime factors.

Factor 30 into any 2 factors.

$3 \cdot 10$	Now factor the 10.
$3 \cdot 2 \cdot 5$	These are the same prime factors even though the original factors were different.

Example: Factor 240 into prime factors.

Factor 240 into any 2 factors.

24 · 10	Now factor both 24 and 10.
4 · 6 · 2 · 5	Now factor both 4 and 6.
2 · 2 · 2 · 3 · 2 · 5	These are prime factors.

This can also be written as $2^4 \cdot 3 \cdot 5$

Divisibility Tests

a. A number is divisible by 2 if that number is an even number (which means it ends in 0,2,4,6 or 8).

1,354 ends in 4, so it is divisible by 2. 240,685 ends in a 5, so it is not divisible by 2.

b. A number is divisible by 3 if the sum of its digits is evenly divisible by 3.

The sum of the digits of 964 is 9+6+4 = 19. Since 19 is not divisible by 3, neither is 964. The digits of 86,514 is 8+6+5+1+4 = 24. Since 24 is divisible by 3, 86,514 is also divisible by 3.

c. A number is divisible by 4 if the number in its last 2 digits is evenly divisible by 4.

The number 113,336 ends with the number 36 in the last 2 columns. Since 36 is divisible by 4, then 113,336 is also divisible by 4.

The number 135,627 ends with the number 27 in the last 2 columns. Since 27 is not evenly divisible by 4, then 135,627 is also not divisible by 4.

d. A number is divisible by 5 if the number ends in either a 5 or a 0. 225 ends with a 5 so it is divisible by 5. The number 470 is also divisible by 5 because its last digit is a 0. 2,358 is not divisible by 5 because its last digit is an 8, not a 5 or a 0.

e. A number is divisible by 6 if the number is even and the sum of its digits is evenly divisible by 3.

4,950 is an even number and its digits add to 18. (4+9+5+0 = 18) Since the number is even and the sum of its digits is 18 (which is divisible by 3), then 4950 is divisible by 6. 326 is an even number, but its digits add up to 11. Since 11 is not divisible by 3, then 326 is not divisible by 6. 698,135 is not an even number, so it cannot possibly be divided evenly by 6.

f. A number is divisible by 8 if the number in its last 3 digits is evenly divisible by 8.

The number 113,336 ends with the 3-digit number 336 in the last 3 places. Since 336 is divisible by 8, then 113,336 is also divisible by 8.
The number 465,627 ends with the number 627 in the last 3 places. Since 627 is not evenly divisible by 8, then 465,627 is also not divisible by 8.

g. A number is divisible by 9 if the sum of its digits is evenly divisible by 9.

The sum of the digits of 874 is 8+7+4 = 19. Since 19 is not divisible by 9, neither is 874. The digits of 116,514 is 1+1+6+5+1+4 = 18. Since 18 is divisible by 9, 116,514 is also divisible by 9.

h. A number is divisible by 10 if the number ends in the digit 0.

305 ends with a 5 so it is not divisible by 10. The number 2,030,270 is divisible by 10 because its last digit is a 0. 42,978 is not divisible by 10 because its last digit is an 8, not a 0.

i. Why these rules work.

All even numbers are divisible by 2 by definition. A 2-digit number (with T as the tens digit and U as the ones digit) has as its sum of the digits, T + U. Suppose this sum of T + U is divisible by 3. Then it equals 3 times some constant, K. So, T + U = 3K. Solving this for U, U = 3K - T. The original 2 digit number would be represented by 10T + U. Substituting 3K - T in place of U, this 2-digit number becomes 10T + U = 10T + (3K - T) = 9T + 3K. This 2-digit number is clearly divisible by 3, since each term is divisible by 3. Therefore, if the sum of the digits of a number is divisible by 3, then the number itself is also divisible by 3. Since 4 divides evenly into 100, 200, or 300, 4 will divide evenly into any amount of hundreds. The only part of a number that determines if 4 will divide into it evenly is the number in the last 2 places. Numbers divisible by 5 end in 5 or 0. This is clear if you look at the answers to the multiplication table for 5. Answers to the multiplication table for 6 are all even numbers. Since 6 factors into 2 times 3, the divisibility rules for 2 and 3 must both work. Any number of thousands is divisible by 8. Only the last 3 places of the number determine whether or not it is divisible by 8. A 2 digit number (with T as the tens digit and U as the ones digit) has as its sum of the digits, T + U. Suppose this sum of T + U is divisible by 9. Then it equals 9 times some constant, K. So, T + U = 9K. Solving this for U, U = 9K - T. The original 2-digit number would be represented by 10T + U. Substituting 9K - T in place of U, this 2-digit number becomes 10T + U = 10T + (9K - T) = 9T + 9K. This 2-digit number is clearly divisible by 9, since each term is divisible by 9. Therefore, if the sum of the digits of a number is divisible by 9, then the number itself is also divisible by 9. Numbers divisible by 10 must be multiples of 10 which all end in a zero.

For standardization purposes, there is an accepted order in which operations are performed in any given algebraic expression. The following pneumonic is often used for the order in which operations are performed.

Please	Parentheses	
Excuse	Exponents	
My	Multiply	Multiply or Divide depending on which operation is encountered first from left to right.
Dear	Divide	
Aunt	Add	Add or Subtract depending on which operation is encountered first from left to right.
Sally	Subtract	

The **exponent form** is a shortcut method to write repeated multiplication. The **base** is the factor. The **exponent** tells how many times that number is multiplied by itself.

The following are basic rules for exponents:

$a^1 = a$ for all values of a; thus $17^1 = 17$

$b^0 = 1$ for all values of b; thus $24^0 = 1$

$10^n = 1$ with n zeros; thus $10^6 = 1,000,000$

To change a number into **scientific notation**, move the decimal point so that only a single digit is to the left of the decimal point. Drop off any trailing zeros. Multiply this number times 10 to a power. The power is the number of positions that the decimal point is moved. The power is negative if the original number is a decimal number between 1 and -1. Otherwise the power is positive.

Example: Change into scientific notation:

4,380,000,000	Move decimal behind the 4
4.38	Drop trailing zeros.
$4.38 \times 10^?$	Count positions that the decimal point has moved.
4.38×10^9	This is the answer.
$-.0000407$	Move decimal behind the 4
-4.07	Count positions that the decimal point has moved.
-4.07×10^{-5}	Note negative exponent.

If a number is already in scientific notation, it can be changed back into regular decimal form. If the exponent on the number 10 is negative, move the decimal point to the left that number of places.. If the exponent on the number 10 is positive, move the decimal point to the right.

Example: Change back into decimal form:

3.448×10^{-2} Move decimal point 2 places left, since exponent is negative.

.03448   This is the answer.

6×10^{4} Move decimal point 4 places right, since exponent is positive.

60,000   This is the answer.

To add or subtract in scientific notation, the exponents must be the same. Then add the decimal portions, keeping the power of 10 the same. Then move the decimal point and adjust the exponent to keep the number to the left of the decimal point to a single digit.

Example:

6.22×10^{3}

$+ 7.48 \times 10^{3}$ Add these as is.

$\overline{13.70 \times 10^{3}}$ Now move decimal 1 more place to the left and

1.37×10^{4} add 1 more exponent.

To multiply or divide in scientific notation, multiply or divide the decimal part of the numbers. In multiplication, add the exponents of 10. In division, subtract the exponents of 10. Then move the decimal point and adjust the exponent to keep the number to the left of the decimal point to a single digit.

Example:

$(5.2 \times 10^{5})(3.5 \times 10^{2})$ Multiply $5.2 \cdot 3.5$

18.2×10^{7} Add exponent

1.82×10^{8} Move decimal point and increase the exponent by 1.

<u>Example:</u>

$$\frac{(4.1076 \times 10^3)}{2.8 \times 10^{-4}}$$ Divide 4.1076 by 2.8

Subtract $3 - (^-4)$

1.467×10^7

Complex numbers can be written in the form $a + bi$ where i represents $\sqrt{-1}$ and a and b are real numbers. a is the real part of the complex number and b is the imaginary part.

If $b = 0$, then the number has no imaginary part and it is a real number.

If $b \neq 0$, then the number is imaginary.

Complex numbers are found when trying to solve equations with negative square roots.

<u>Example:</u> If $x^2 + 9 = 0$
then $x^2 = -9$
and $x = \sqrt{-9}$ or $+3i$ and $-3i$

a.   **Natural numbers**—the counting numbers, $1, 2, 3, ...$

b.   **Whole numbers**—the counting numbers along with zero, $0, 1, 2...$

c.   **Integers**—the counting numbers, their opposites, and zero, ..., $^-1, 0, 1, ...$

d.   **Rationals**—all of the fractions that can be formed from the whole numbers. Zero cannot be the denominator. In decimal form, these numbers will either be terminating or repeating decimals. Simplify square roots to determine if the number can be written as a fraction.

e.   **Irrationals**—real numbers that cannot be written as a fraction. The decimal forms of these numbers are neither terminating nor repeating. Examples: $\pi, e, \sqrt{2}$, etc.

f.   **Real numbers**—the set of numbers obtained by combining the rationals and irrationals. Complex numbers, i.e. numbers that involve i or $\sqrt{-1}$ [SA7], are not real numbers.

The **Denseness Property** of real numbers states that, if all real numbers are ordered from least to greatest on a number line, there is an infinite set of real numbers between any two given numbers on the line.

Example:

Between 7.6 and 7.7, there is the rational number 7.65 in the set of real numbers.

Between 3 and 4 there exists no other natural number.

Number Sets

Set A - - $\left\{ ^-5, ^-3, 0, 1, 2, 3, 5 \right\}$

Set B - - $\left\{ ^-7, ^-2, 0, 1, 3, 4, 5, 6 \right\}$

Set C - - $\left\{ ^-6, ^-4, ^-2, 4, 6 \right\}$

The **Union** ($\cup$) of two sets is the set of all the numbers which are either in the first set or the second set or both sets.

$$A \cup B \text{ is } \left\{ ^-7, ^-5, ^-3, ^-2, 0, 1, 2, 3, 4, 5, 6 \right\}.$$

The **Intersection** ($\cap$) of two sets is the set of numbers that are in both sets.
$$A \cap B \text{ is } \left\{ 0, 1, 3, 5 \right\}.$$

The **Null Set** is also called the empty set; it is the set that does not contain any numbers. The Null Set can be expressed two different ways: either { } or $\varnothing$. {0} is NOT the Null Set since it does have one element.

A $\cap$ C is the empty set, { }, since they do not share any elements.

SUBAREA II.   **RELATIONS, FUNCTIONS, AND ALGEBRA**

Competency 0005   Understand mathematical patterns and use them to solve problems.

When given a set of numbers where the common difference between the terms is constant, use the following formula:

$a_n = a_1 + (n - 1)d$, where

> a_1 = the first term
> a_n = the nth term (general term)
> d = the common difference

Example:
Find the 8th term of the arithmetic sequence 5, 8, 11, 14...

$a_n = a_1 + (n-1)d$	
$a_1 = 5$	identify the 1st term
$d = 8 - 5 = 3$	find d
$a_n = 5 + (8-1)3$	substitute
$a_n = 26$	

Example:
Given two terms of an arithmetic sequence, find a_1 and d.
$a_4 = 21$ $a_6 = 32$
$a_n = a_1 + (n-1)d$ $a_4 = 21, n = 4$
$21 = a_1 + (4-1)d$ $a_6 = 32, n = 6$
$32 = a_1 + (6-1)d$

$21 = a_1 + 3d$ solve the system of equations
$32 = a_1 + 5d$

$32 = a_1 + 5d$
$\underline{-21 = -a_1 - 3d}$ multiply by –1
$11 = 2d$ add the equations

$5.5 = d$

$21 = a_1 + 3(5.5)$ substitute d = 5.5 into one of the equations
$21 = a_1 + 16.5$
$a_1 = 4.5$

The sequence begins with 4.5 and has a common difference of 5.5 between numbers.

Geometric Sequences

When using geometric sequences, consecutive numbers are compared to find the common ratio.

$$r = \frac{a_{n+1}}{a_n} \text{ where}$$

r = common ratio
a_n = the nth term

The ratio is then used in the geometric sequence formula:
$a_n = a_1 r^{n-1}$

Example:
Find the 8th term of the geometric sequence 2, 8, 32, 128...

$r = \dfrac{a_{n+1}}{a_n}$ use common ratio formula to find ratio

$r = \dfrac{8}{2}$ substitute $a_n = 2$, $a_{n+1} = 8$

$r = 4$

$a_n = a_1 \bullet r^{n-1}$ use $r = 4$ to solve for the 8th term
$a_n = 2 \bullet 4^{8-1}$
$a_n = 32,768$

The sums of terms in a progression is simply found by determining if it is an arithmetic or geometric sequence and then using the appropriate formula.

Sum of first n terms of an arithmetic sequence.

$$S_n = \frac{n}{2}(a_1 + a_n)$$

or

$$S_n = \frac{n}{2}\left[2a_1 + (n-1)d\right]$$

Sum of first n terms of a geometric sequence.

$$S_n = \frac{a_1(r^n - 1)}{r - 1}, r \neq 1$$

Sample Problems:

1. $\displaystyle\sum_{i=1}^{10}(2i + 2)$

This means find the sum of the terms beginning with the first term and ending with the 10th term of the sequence $a = 2i + 2$.

$a_1 = 2(1) + 2 = 4$

$a_{10} = 2(10) + 2 = 22$

$S_n = \frac{n}{2}(a_1 + a_n)$

$S_n = \frac{10}{2}(4 + 22)$

$S_n = 130$

1. Find the sum of the first 6 terms in an arithmetic sequence if the first term is 2 and the common difference, d is-3.

$n = 6 \qquad a_1 = 2 \qquad d = {}^-3$

$S_n = \frac{n}{2}\left[2a_1 + (n-1)d\right]$

$S_6 = \frac{6}{2}\left[2\times 2 + (6-1){}^-3\right]$ Substitute known values.

$S_6 = 3\left[4 + \left({}^-15\right)\right]$ Solve.

$S_6 = 3(-11) = -33$

3. Find $\displaystyle\sum_{i=1}^{5} 4 \times 2^{i}$

This means the sum of the first 5 terms where $a_i = a \times b^i$ and $r = b$.

$a_1 = 4 \times 2^1 = 8$

Identify a_1, r, n

$r = 2 \qquad n = 5$

$S_n = \dfrac{a_1(r^n - 1)}{r - 1}$

Substitute a, r, n

$S_5 = \dfrac{8(2^5 - 1)}{2 - 1}$

Solve.

$S_5 = \dfrac{8(31)}{1} = 248$

Practice problems:

1. Find the sum of the first five terms of the sequence if $a = 7$ and $d = 4$.

2. $\displaystyle\sum_{i=1}^{7}(2i - 4)$

3. $\displaystyle\sum_{i=1}^{6} {}^{-}3\left(\dfrac{2}{5}\right)^{i}$

The **iterative process** involves repeated use of the same steps. A **recursive function** is an example of the iterative process. A recursive function is a function that requires the computation of all previous terms in order to find a subsequent term. Perhaps the most famous recursive function is the **Fibonacci sequence**. This is the sequence of numbers 1,1,2,3,5,8,13,21,34 … for which the next term is found by adding the previous two terms.

Competency 0006 **Understand the principles and properties of algebraic relations and functions, including inverses and compositions.**

- A **relation** is any set of ordered pairs.

- The **domain** of a relation is the set made of all the first coordinates of the ordered pairs.

- The **range** of a relation is the set made of all the second coordinates of the ordered pairs.

- A **function** is a relation in which different ordered pairs have different first coordinates. (No x values are repeated.)

- A **mapping** is a diagram with arrows drawn from each element of the domain to the corresponding elements of the range. If 2 arrows are drawn from the same element of the domain, then it is not a function.

- On a graph, use the **vertical line test** to look for a function. If any vertical line intersects the graph of a relation in more than one point, then the relation is not a function.

1. Determine the domain and range of this mapping.

ANSWERS

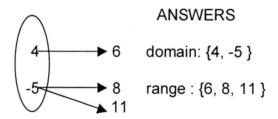

domain: {4, -5 }

range : {6, 8, 11 }

2. Determine which of these are functions:

    a. $\{(1,^-4),(27,1)(94,5)(2,^-4)\}$

    b. $f(x) = 2x - 3$

    c. $A = \{(x,y) \mid xy = 24\}$

    d. $y = 3$

    e. $x = {}^-9$

    f. $\{(3,2),(7,7),(0,5),(2,^-4),(8,^-6),(1,0),(5,9),(6,^-4)\}$

3. Determine the domain and range of this graph.

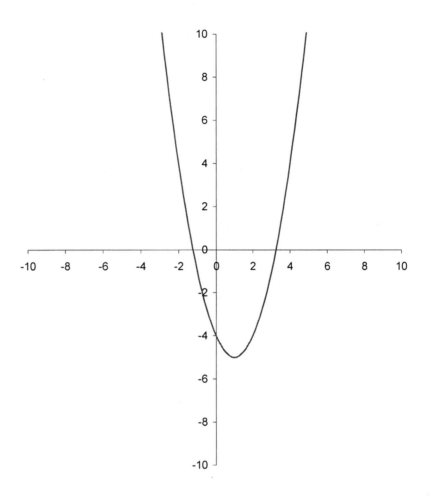

4. If $A = \{(x, y) \mid y = x^2 - 6\}$, find the domain and range.

5. Give the domain and range of set B if:

$$B = \{(1, ^-2), (4, ^-2), (7, ^-2), (6, ^-2)\}$$

6. Determine the domain of this function:

$$f(x) = \frac{5x + 7}{x^2 - 4}$$

7. Determine the domain and range of these graphs.

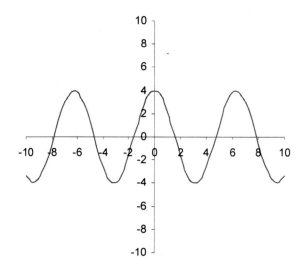

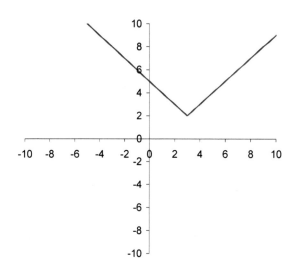

8. If $E = \{(x, y) \mid y = 5\}$, find the domain and range.

9. Determine the ordered pairs in the relation shown in this mapping.

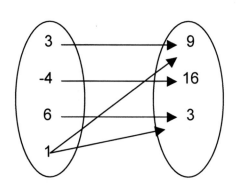

A function can be defined as a set of ordered pairs in which each element of the domain is paired with one and only one element of the range. The symbol $f(x)$ is read "f of x." Letter other than "f" can be used to represent a function. The letter "g" is commonly used as in $g(x)$.

Sample problems:

1. Given $f(x) = 4x^2 - 2x + 3$, find $f(^-3)$.

(This question is asking for the range value that corresponds to the domain value of $^-3$).

$$f(x) = 4x^2 - 2x + 3$$
$$f(^-3) = 4(^-3)^2 - 2(^-3) + 3$$
$$f(^-3) = 45$$

1. Replace x with $^-3$.

2. Solve.

2. Find $f(3)$ and $f(10)$, given $f(x) = 7$.

$$f(x) = 7$$
$$(3) = 7$$

1. There are no x values to substitute for. This is your answer.

$$f(x) = 7$$
$$f10) = 7$$

2. Same as above.

Notice that both answers are equal to the constant given.

Competency 0007 Understand the properties of linear functions and relations.

When **graphing a first-degree equation**, solve for the variable. The graph of this solution will be a single point on the number line. There will be no arrows.

When graphing a linear inequality, the dot will be hollow if the inequality sign is < or >. If the inequality signs is either ≥ or ≤, the dot on the graph will be solid. The arrow goes to the right for ≥ or >. The arrow goes to the left for < or ≤.

Example: $5(x + 2) + 2x = 3(x - 2)$
$$5x + 10 + 2x = 3x - 6$$
$$7x + 10 = 3x - 6$$
$$4x = -16$$
$$x = -4$$

Example: $2(3x - 7) > 10x - 2$
$$6x - 14 > 10x - 2$$
$$-4x > 12$$
$$x < -3$$

[SA8]

Practice Problems:

1. $5x - 1 > 14$
2. $7(2x - 3) + 5x = 19 - x$
3. $3x + 42 \geq 12x - 12$
4. $5 - 4(x + 3) = 9$

A first degree equation can be written in the form $ax + by = c$. To graph this equation, find either one point and the slope of the line, or find two points. To find a point and slope, solve the equation for y. This gets the equation in the **slope-intercept form**, $y = mx + b$. The point $(0,b)$ is the y-intercept and m is the line's slope.

To find two points, substitute any number for x, then solve for y. Repeat this with a different number. To find the intercepts, substitute 0 for x and then 0 for y.

Remember that graphs will go up as they go to the right when the slope is positive. Negative slopes make the lines go down as they go to the right.

If the equation solves to $x = $ a constant, then the graph is a **vertical line**. It only has an x- intercept. Its slope is undefined.

If the equation solves to $y = $ a constant, then the graph is a **horizontal line**. It only has a y-intercept. Its slope is 0 (zero).

When graphing a linear inequality, the line will be dotted if the inequality sign is $<$ or $>$. If the inequality signs are either $\leq$ or $\geq$, the line on the graph will be a solid line.

Shade above the line when the inequality sign is $>$ or $\geq$. Shade below the line when the inequality sign is $<$ or$\leq$. For inequalities of the form $x > k$, $x \geq k$, $x < k$, or $x \leq k$

where k = any number, the graph will be a vertical line (solid or dotted.) Shade to the right for $>$ or $\geq$. Shade to the left for $<$ or $\leq$. Remember: Dividing or multiplying by a negative number will reverse the direction of the inequality sign.

Examples:

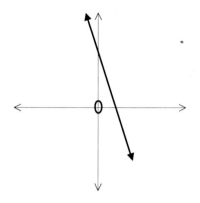

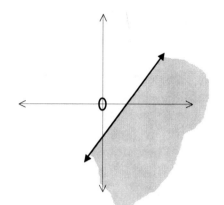

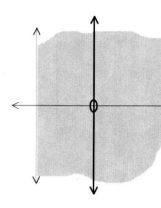

$5x + 2y = 6$

$y = -\dfrac{5}{2}x + 3$

$3x - 2y \geq 6$

$y \leq \dfrac{3}{2}x - 3$

$3x + 12 > -3$

$x > -5$

Graph the following:

1. $2x - y = {}^-4$
2. $x + 3y > 6$
3. $3x + 2y \leq 2y - 6$

- A **first degree equation** has an equation of the form $ax + by = c$. To find the slope of a line, solve the equation for y. This gets the equation into **slope intercept form:** $y = mx + b$. The value m is the line's slope.

- To find the y intercept, substitute 0 for x and solve for y. This is the y intercept. The y intercept is also the value of b in $y = mx + b$.

- To find the x intercept, substitute 0 for y and solve for x. This is the x intercept.

- If the equation solves to x = **any number**, then the graph is a **vertical line**. It only has an x intercept. Its slope is **undefined**.

- If the equation solves to y = **any number**, then the graph is a **horizontal line**. It only has a y intercept. Its slope is 0 (zero).

1. Find the slope and intercepts of $3x + 2y = 14$.

$$3x + 2y = 14$$
$$2y = {}^-3x + 14$$
$$y = {}^-3/2\ x + 7$$

The slope of the line is ${}^-3/2$, the value of m.
The y intercept of the line is 7.

The intercepts can also be found by substituting 0 in place of the other variable in the equation.

To find the y intercept:
let $x = 0$; $3(0) + 2y = 14$
$0 + 2y = 14$
$2y = 14$
$y = 7$
$(0,7)$ is the y intercept.

To find the x intercept:
let $y = 0$; $3x + 2(0) = 14$
$3x + 0 = 14$
$3x = 14$
$x = 14/3$
$(14/3, 0)$ is the x intercept.

Find the slope and the intercepts (if they exist) for these equations:

1. $5x + 7y = -70$
2. $x - 2y = 14$
3. $5x + 3y = 3(5 + y)$
4. $2x + 5y = 15$

- The **equation of a graph** can be found by finding its slope and its y intercept. To find the slope, find 2 points on the graph where co-ordinates are integer values. Using points: (x_1, y_1) and (x_2, y_2).

$$\text{slope} = \frac{y_2 - y_1}{x_2 - x_1}$$

The y intercept is the y coordinate of the point where a line crosses the y axis. The equation can be written in slope-intercept form, which is $y = mx + b$, where m is the slope and b is the y intercept. To rewrite the equation into some other form, multiply each term by the common denominator of all the fractions. Then rearrange terms as necessary.

- If the graph is a **vertical line**, then the equation solves to x = **the** x **co-ordinate of any point on the line**.

- If the graph is a **horizontal line**, then the equation solves to y = **the** y **coordinate of any point on the line**.

- Given two points on a line, the first thing to do is to find the **slope of the line**. If 2 points on the graph are (x_1, y_1) and (x_2, y_2), then the slope is found using the formula:

$$\text{slope} = \frac{y_2 - y_1}{x_2 - x_1}$$

The slope will now be denoted by the letter **m**. To write the equation of a line, choose either point. Substitute them into the formula:

$$Y - y_a = m(X - x_a)$$

Remember (x_a, y_a) can be (x_1, y_1) or (x_2, y_2) If **m**, the value of the slope, is distributed through the parentheses, the equation can be rewritten into other forms of the equation of a line.

Find the equation of a line through $(9, {}^-6)$ and $({}^-1, 2)$.

$$\text{slope} = \frac{y_2 - y_1}{x_2 - x_1} = \frac{2 - {}^-6}{{}^-1 - 9} = \frac{8}{{}^-10} = -\frac{4}{5}$$

$$Y - y_a = m(X - x_a) \rightarrow Y - 2 = {}^-4/5(X - {}^-1) \rightarrow$$
$$Y - 2 = {}^-4/5(X + 1) \rightarrow Y - 2 = {}^-4/5\,X - 4/5 \rightarrow$$
$$Y = {}^-4/5\,X + 6/5 \quad \text{This is the slope-intercept form.}$$

Multiplying by 5 to eliminate fractions, it is:

$$5Y = {}^-4X + 6 \rightarrow 4X + 5Y = 6 \quad \text{Standard form.}$$

Write the equation of a line through these two points:

1. $(5, 8)$ and $({}^-3, 2)$
2. $(11, 10)$ and $(11, {}^-3)$
3. $({}^-4, 6)$ and $(6, 12)$
4. $(7, 5)$ and $({}^-3, 5)$

Competency 0008   Understand the properties of quadratic and higher-order polynomial functions and relations.

To factor a polynomial, follow these steps:

a. **Factor out any GCF** (greatest common factor)

b. For a binomial (2 terms), check to see if the problem is the **difference of perfect squares**. If both factors are perfect squares, then it factors this way:

$$a^2 - b^2 = (a-b)(a+b)$$

If the problem is not the difference of perfect squares, then check to see if the problem is either the sum or difference of perfect cubes.

$$x^3 - 8y^3 = (x - 2y)(x^2 + 2xy + 4y^2) \qquad \leftarrow \text{difference}$$

[SA9]

$$64a^3 + 27b^3 = (4a + 3b)(16a^2 - 12ab + 9b^2) \qquad \leftarrow \text{sum}$$

[SA10]c. Trinomials can be perfect squares. Trinomials can be factored into 2 binomials (un-FOILing). Be sure the terms of the trinomial are in descending order. If the last sign of the trinomial is a "+," then the signs in the parentheses will be the same as the sign in front of the second term of the trinomial. If the last sign of the trinomial is a "−," then there will be one "+" and one "−" in the two parentheses. The first term of the trinomial can be factored to equal the first terms of the two factors. The last term of the trinomial can be factored to equal the last terms of the two factors. Work backwards to determine the correct factors to multiply together to get the correct center term.

Factor completely:

1. $4x^2 - 25y^2$ [SA11]
2. $6b^2 - 2b - 8$

Answers:

1. No GCF; this is the difference of perfect squares.

$$4x^2 - 25y^2 = (2x - 5y)(2x + 5y)$$

2. GCF of 2; Try to factor into 2 binomials:

$$6b^2 - 2b - 8 = 2(3b^2 - b - 4)$$

Since the last sign of the trinomial is a "−," the signs in the factors are one "+," and one "−." $3b^2$ factors into $3b$ and b. Find factors of 4: 1 & 4; 2 & 2.

$$6b^2 - 2b - 8 = 2(3b^2 - b - 4) = 2(3b - 4)(b + 1)$$

A **quadratic equation** is written in the form $ax^2 + bx + c = 0$. To solve a quadratic equation by factoring, at least one of the factors must equal zero.

Example:
Solve the equation.

$x^2 + 10x - 24 = 0$
$(x + 12)(x - 2) = 0$ Factor.
$x + 12 = 0$ or $x - 2 = 0$ Set each factor equal to 0.

$x = {}^-12$ $x = 2$ Solve.

Check:
$x^2 + 10x - 24 = 0$

$({}^-12)^2 + 10({}^-12) - 24 = 0$ $(2)^2 + 10(2) - 24 = 0$
$144 - 120 - 24 = 0$ $4 + 20 - 24 = 0$
$0 = 0$ $0 = 0$

Example:

Graph $y = 3x^2 + x - 2$.

x	$y = 3x^2 + x - 2$
-2	8
-1	0
0	-2
1	2
2	12

[SA12]

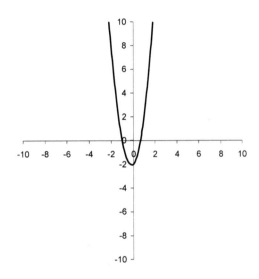

To solve a quadratic equation using the **quadratic formula**, be sure that your equation is in the form $ax^2 + bx + c = 0$. Substitute these values into the formula:

$$x = \frac{-b \pm \sqrt{b^2 - 4ac}}{2a}$$

Example:

Solve the equation.

$$3x^2 = 7 + 2x \rightarrow 3x^2 - 2x - 7 = 0$$
$$a = 3 \quad b = -2 \quad c = -7$$

$$x = \frac{-(-2) \pm \sqrt{(-2)^2 - 4(3)(-7)}}{2(3)}$$

$$x = \frac{2 \pm \sqrt{4 + 84}}{6}$$

$$x = \frac{2 \pm \sqrt{88}}{6}$$

$$x = \frac{2 \pm 2\sqrt{22}}{6}$$

$$x = \frac{1 \pm \sqrt{22}}{3}$$

Follow these steps to write a quadratic equation from its roots:

1. Add the roots together. The answer is their **sum**. Multiply the roots together. The answer is their **product**.
2. A quadratic equation can be written using the sum and product like this:

$$x^2 + \textbf{(opposite of the sum)}x + \textbf{product} = 0$$

3. If there are any fractions in the equation, multiply every term by the common denominator to eliminate the fractions. This is the quadratic equation.
4. If a quadratic equation has only 1 root, use it twice and follow the first 3 steps above.

Example:
Find a quadratic equation with roots of 4 and $^-9$.

Solutions:
The sum of 4 and $^-9$ is $^-5$. The product of 4 and $^-9$ is $^-36$. The equation would be:

$$x^2 + \textbf{(opposite of the sum)}x + \textbf{product} = 0$$
$$x^2 + 5x - 36 = 0$$

Find a quadratic equation with roots of $5 + 2i$ and $5 - 2i$.

Solutions:
The sum of $5 + 2i$ and $5 - 2i$ is 10. The product of $5 + 2i$ and $5 - 2i$ is $25 - 4i^2 = 25 + 4 = 29$.

The equation would be:

$$x^2 + \textbf{(opposite of the sum)}x + \textbf{product} = 0$$
$$x^2 - 10x + 29 = 0$$

Find a quadratic equation with roots of $2/3$ and $^-3/4$.

Solutions:
The sum of $2/3$ and $^-3/4$ is $^-1/12$. The product of $2/3$ and $^-3/4$ is $^-1/2$.

The equation would be :

$$x^2 + \textbf{(opposite of the sum)}x + \textbf{product} = 0$$
$$x^2 + 1/12\, x - 1/2 = 0$$

Common denominator = 12, so multiply by 12.

$$12(x^2 + 1/12\, x - 1/2 = 0$$
$$12x^2 + 1x - 6 = 0$$
$$12x^2 + x - 6 = 0$$

Try these:

1. Find a quadratic equation with a root of 5.
2. Find a quadratic equation with roots of $8/5$ and $^-6/5$.
3. Find a quadratic equation with roots of 12 and $^-3$.

To graph an inequality, **graph the quadratic** as if it was an equation; however, if the inequality has just a $>$ or $<$ sign, then make the curve itself dotted. Shade above the curve for $>$ or $\geq$. Shade below the curve for $<$ or $\leq$.

Examples:

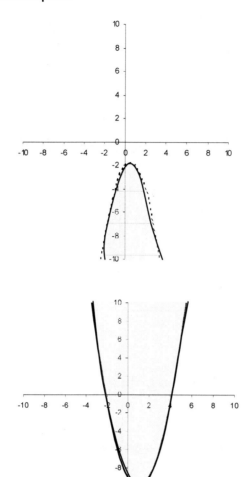

To graph an inequality, **solve the inequality** for y. This gets the inequality in **slope intercept form**, (for example $y < mx + b$). The point (0, b) is the y-intercept and m is the line's slope.

If the inequality solves to $x \geq$ **any number**, then the graph includes a **vertical line**.

If the inequality solves to $y \leq$ **any number**, then the graph includes a **horizontal line**.

When graphing a linear inequality, the line will be dotted if the inequality sign is $<$ or $>$. If the inequality signs are either $\geq$ or $\leq$, the line on the graph will be a solid line. Shade above the line when the inequality sign is $\geq$ or $>$. Shade below the line when the inequality sign is $<$ or $\leq$. For inequalities of the forms $x >$ number, $x \leq$ number, $x <$ number, or $x \geq$ number, draw a vertical line (solid or dotted). Shade to the right for $>$ or $\geq$. Shade to the left for $<$ or $\leq$.

Use these rules to graph and shade each inequality. The solution to a system of linear inequalities consists of the part of the graph that is shaded for each inequality. For instance, if the graph of one inequality is shaded with red, and the graph of another inequality is shaded with blue, then the overlapping area would be shaded purple. The purple area would be the points in the solution set of this system.

Example: Solve by graphing:

$$x + y \leq 6$$
$$x - 2y \leq 6$$

Solving the inequalities for y, they become:

$$y \leq -x + 6 \text{ [SA13]} \quad (y\text{-intercept of 6 and slope} = -1)$$
$$y \geq 1/2 x - 3 \quad (y \text{ intercept of } -3 \text{ and slope} = 1/2)$$

A graph with shading is shown below:

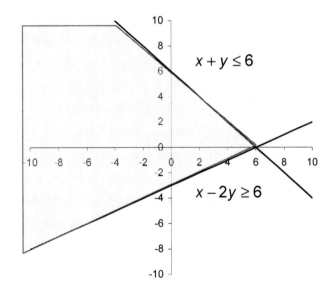

To solve a **quadratic equation** (with x^2), rewrite the equation into the form:

$$ax^2 + bx + c = 0 \quad \text{or} \quad y = ax^2 + bx + c$$

where a, b, and c are real numbers. Then substitute the values of a, b, and c into the quadratic formula:

$$x = \frac{-b \pm \sqrt{b^2 - 4ac}}{2a}$$

Simplify the result to find the answers. (Remember, there could be 2 real answers, one real answer, or 2 complex answers that include "i").

To solve a quadratic inequality (with x^2), solve for y. The axis of symmetry is located at $x = -b/2a$. Find coordinates of points to each side of the axis of symmetry. Graph the parabola as a dotted line if the inequality sign is either $<$ or $>$. Graph the parabola as a solid line if the inequality sign is either $\leq$ or $\geq$. Shade above the parabola if the sign is $\geq$ or $>$. Shade below the parabola if the sign is $\leq$ or $<$.

Example: Solve: $8x^2 - 10x - 3 = 0$

In this equation $a = 8$, $b = -10$, and $c = -3$.
Substituting these into the quadratic equation, it becomes:

$$x = \frac{-(-10) \pm \sqrt{(-10)^2 - 4(8)(-3)}}{2(8)} = \frac{10 \pm \sqrt{100 + 96}}{16}$$

$$x = \frac{10 \pm \sqrt{196}}{16} = \frac{10 \pm 14}{16} = \frac{24}{16} \, or \, \frac{-4}{16} = \frac{3}{2} \, or \, -\frac{1}{4}$$

Check:

$$x = -\frac{1}{4}$$

$$\frac{1}{2} + \frac{10}{4} - 3 = 0 \qquad \text{Both Check}$$

$$3 - 3 = 0$$

Example: Solve and graph : $y > x^2 + 4x - 5$.

The axis of symmetry is located at $x = {}^-b/2a$. Substituting 4 for b, and 1 for a, this formula becomes:

$$x = {}^-(4)/2(1) = {}^-4/2 = {}^-2$$

Find coordinates of points to each side of $x = {}^-2$.

x	y
⁻5	0
⁻4	⁻5
⁻3	⁻8
⁻2	⁻9
⁻1	⁻8
0	⁻5
1	0

Graph these points to form a parabola. Draw it as a dotted line. Since a greater than sign is used, shade above and inside the parabola.

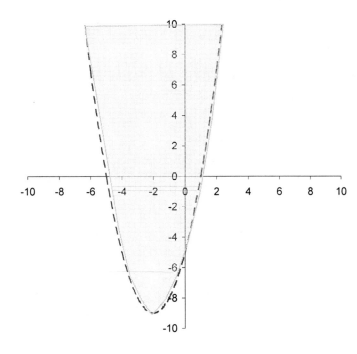

Conic sections result from the intersection of a cone and a plane. The three main types of conics are parabolas, ellipses, and hyperbolas.

The general equation for a conic section is:

$$Ax^2 + Bxy + Cy^2 + Dx + Ey + F = 0$$

The value of $B^2 - 4AC$ determines the type of conic. If $B^2 - 4AC$ is less than zero the curve is an ellipse or a circle. If equal to zero, the curve is a parabola. If greater than zero, the curve is a hyperbola.

The equation of a circle with its center at (h, k) and a radius r units is:

$$(x - h)^2 + (y - k)^2 = r^2$$

Sample Problem:

1. Given the equation $x^2 + y^2 = 9$, find the center and the radius of the circle. Then graph the equation.

First, writing the equation in standard circle form gives:

$$(x - 0)^2 + (y - 0)^2 = 3^2$$

Therefore, the center is (0,0) and the radius is 3 units.

Sketch the circle:

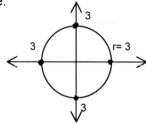

2. Given the equation $x^2 + y^2 - 3x + 8y - 20 = 0$, find the center and the radius. Then graph the circle.

First, write the equation in standard circle form by completing the square for both variables.

$x^2 + y^2 - 3x + 8y - 20 = 0$ 1. Complete the squares.

$(x^2 - 3x + 9/4) + (y^2 + 8y + 16) = 20 + 9/4 + 16$

$(x - 3/2)^2 + (y + 4)^2 = 153/4$

The center is $(3/2, {}^-4)$ and the radius is $\dfrac{\sqrt{153}}{2}$ or $\dfrac{3\sqrt{17}}{2}$.

Graph the circle.

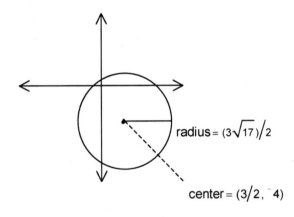

radius $= (3\sqrt{17})/2$

center $= (3/2, {}^-4)$

Competency 0009   Understand the principles and properties of rational, absolute value, exponential, and logarithmic functions.

A **rational function** is given in the form $f(x) = p(x)/q(x)$. In the equation, p(x) and q(x) both represent polynomial functions where q(x) does not equal zero. The branches of rational functions approach asymptotes. Setting the denominator equal to zero and solving will give the value(s) of the vertical asymptotes(s) since the function will be undefined at this point. If the value of f(x) approaches b as the $|x|$ increases, the equation $y = b$ is a horizontal asymptote. To find the horizontal asymptote it is necessary to make a table of values for x that are to the right and left of the vertical asymptotes. The pattern for the horizontal asymptotes will become apparent as the $|x|$ increases.

If there is more than one vertical asymptote, remember to choose numbers to the right and left of each one in order to find the horizontal asymptotes and have sufficient points to graph the function.

Sample problem:

1. Graph $f(x) = \dfrac{3x + 1}{x - 2}$.

$$x - 2 = 0$$
$$x = 2$$

1. Set denominator $= 0$ to find the vertical asymptote.

x	f(x)
3	10
10	3.875
100	3.07
1000	3.007
1	⁻4
⁻10	2.417
⁻100	2.93
⁻1000	2.99

2. Make a table, choosing numbers to the right and left of the vertical asymptote.

3. The pattern shows that as $|x|$ increases, f(x) approaches the value 3; therefore a horizontal asymptote exists at $y = 3$

Sketch the graph.

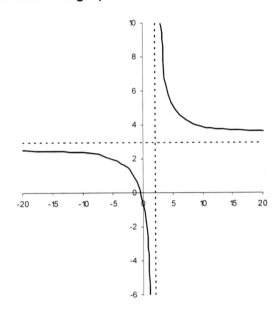

When changing **common logarithms to exponential form**,

$$y = \log_b x \quad \text{if and only if} \quad x = b^y$$

Natural logarithms can be changed to exponential form by using,

$$\log_e x = \ln x \quad \text{or} \quad \ln x = y \quad \text{can be written as} \quad e^y = x$$

Practice Problems:

Express in exponential form.

1. $\log_3 81 = 4$
   $x = 81 \quad b = 3 \quad y = 4$ Identify values.
   $81 = 3^4$ Rewrite in exponential form.

Solve by writing in exponential form.

2. $\log_x 125 = 3$

   $x^3 = 125$ Write in exponential form.
   $x^3 = 5^3$ Write 125 in exponential form.
   $x = 5$ Bases must be equal if exponents are equal.

Use a scientific calculator to solve.

3. Find $\ln 72$.

   $\ln 72 = 4.2767$ Use the $\ln x$ key to find natural logs.

4. Find $\ln x = 4.2767$ Write in exponential form.

   $e^{4.2767} = x$ Use the key (or 2nd $\ln x$) to find x.

   $x = 72.002439$ The small difference is due to rounding.

To **solve logarithms or exponential functions** it is necessary to use several properties.

Multiplication Property $\log_b mn = \log_b m + \log_b n$

Quotient Property $\log_b \dfrac{m}{n} = \log_b m - \log_b n$

Powers Property $\log_b n^r = r \log_b n$

Equality Property $\log_b n = \log_b m$ if and only if $n = m$.

Change of Base Formula $\log_b n = \dfrac{\log n}{\log b}$

     $\log_b b^x = x$ and $b^{\log_b x} = x$

Sample problem.

Solve for x.

1. $\log_6 (x - 5) + \log_6 x = 2$

   $\log_6 x(x - 5) = 2$ Use product property.

   $\log_6 x^2 - 5x = 2$ Distribute.

   $x^2 - 5x = 6^2$ Write in exponential form.

   $x^2 - 5x - 36 = 0$ Solve quadratic equation.

   $(x + 4)(x - 9) = 0$

   $x = {}^-4$ $x = 9$

***Be sure to check results. Remember x must be greater than zero in $\log x = y$.

Check: $\log_6(x-5)+\log_6 x = 2$

$\log_6(^-4-5)+\log_6(^-4) = 2$ — Substitute the first answer $^-4$.

$\log_6(^-9)+\log_6(^-4) = 2$ — This is undefined, x is less than zero.

$\log_6(9-5)+\log_6 9 = 2$ — Substitute the second answer 9.

$\log_6 4+\log_6 9 = 2$

$\log_6(4)(9) = 2$ — Multiplication property.

$\log_6 36 = 2$

$6^2 = 36$ — Write in exponential form.

$36 = 36$

Practice problems:

1. $\log_4 x = 2\log_4 3$
2. $2\log_3 x = 2 + \log_3(x-2)$
3. Use change of base formula to find $(\log_3 4)(\log_4 3)$

-The **absolute value function** for a 1st degree equation is of the form:

$y = m(x-h)+k$. Its graph is in the shape of a $\vee$. The point (h,k) is the location of the maximum/minimum point on the graph. "± m" are the slopes of the 2 sides of the $\vee$. The graph opens up if m is positive and down if m is negative.

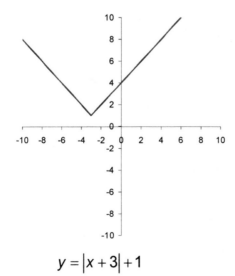

$$y = |x+3|+1$$

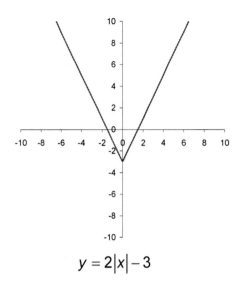

$$y = 2|x| - 3$$

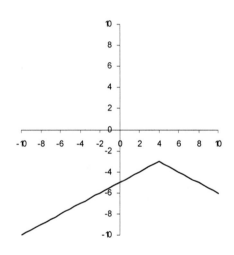

$$y = {}^-1/2|x - 4| - 3$$

-Note that on the first graph above, the graph opens up since m is positive 1. It has ($^-$3,1) as its minimum point. The slopes of the 2 upward rays are $\pm$ 1.

-The second graph also opens up since m is positive. (0, $^-$3) is its minimum point. The slopes of the 2 upward rays are $\pm$ 2.

-The third graph is a downward $\wedge$ because m is $^-$1/2. The maximum point on the graph is at (4, $^-$3). The slopes of the 2 downward rays are $\pm$ 1/2.

-The **identity function** is the linear equation $y = x$. Its graph is a line going through the origin (0,0) and through the first and third quadrants at a $45°$ degree angle.

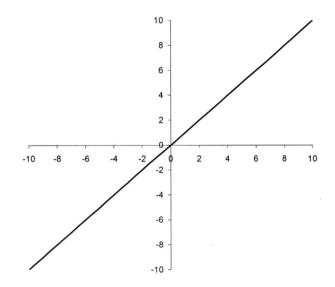

-The **greatest integer function** or **step function** has the equation: $f(x) = j[rx - h] + k$ or $y = j[rx - h] + k$. (h,k) is the location of the left endpoint of one step. j is the vertical jump from step to step. r is the reciprocal of the length of each step. If (x, y) is a point of the function, then when x is an integer, its y value is the same integer. If (x, y) is a point of the function, then when x is not an integer, its y value is the first integer less than x. Points on $y = [x]$ would include:

(3,3), (⁻2,⁻2), (0,0), (1.5,1), (2.83,2), (⁻3.2,⁻4), (⁻.4,⁻1).

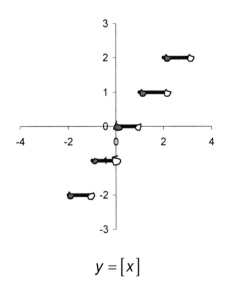

$$y = [x]$$

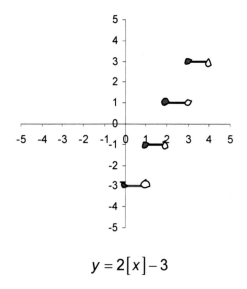

$$y = 2[x] - 3$$

-Note that in the graph of the first equation, the steps are going up as they move to the right.

Each step is one space wide (inverse of r) with a solid dot on the left and a hollow dot on the right where the jump to the next step occurs. Each step is one square higher $(j = 1)$ than the previous step. One step of the graph starts at $(0,0) \leftarrow$ values of (h,k).
-In the second graph, the graph goes up to the right. One step starts at the point $(0, {}^-3) \leftarrow$ values of (h,k). Each step is one square wide $(r = 1)$ and each step is 2 squares higher than the previous step $(j = 2)$.

Practice: Graph the following equations:

1. $f(x) = x$
2. $y = {}^-|x - 3| + 5$
3. $y = 3[x]$
4. $y = 2/5|x - 5| - 2$

SUBAREA III.   **MEASUREMENT AND GEOMETRY**

Competency 0010 **Understand principles and procedures related to measurement.**

The strategy for solving problems of this nature should be to identify the given shapes and choose the correct formulas. Subtract the smaller cut out shape from the larger shape.

Sample problems:

1. Find the area of one side of the metal in the circular flat washer shown below:

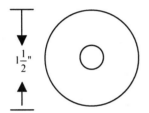

$1\frac{1}{2}"$

1. the shapes are both circles.

2. use the formula $A = \pi r^2$ for both.

   (Inside diameter is $3/8"$ **)**

Area of larger circle   Area of smaller circle

$A = \pi r^2$ $A = \pi r^2$

$A = \pi(.75^2)$ $A = \pi(.1875^2)$

$A = 1.76625$ in^2 $A = .1103906$ in^2 [SA14]

Area of metal washer = larger area - smaller area

$\qquad$ = 1.76625 in^2 − .1103906 in^2 [SA15]

$\qquad$ = 1.6558594 in^2 [SA16]

2. You have decided to fertilize your lawn. The shapes and dimensions of your lot, house, pool and garden are given in the diagram below. The shaded area will not be fertilized. If each bag of fertilizer costs $7.95 and covers 4,500 square feet, find the total number of bags needed and the total cost of the fertilizer.

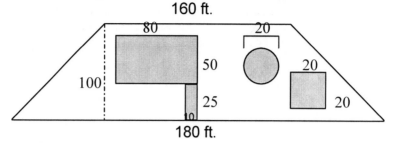

Area of Lot

$A = \frac{1}{2} h(b_1 + b_2)$

$A = \frac{1}{2}(100)(180 + 160)$

$A = 17,000$ sq ft

Area of House

$A = LW$

$A = (80)(50)$

$A = 4,000$ sq ft

Area of Driveway

$A = LW$

$A = (10)(25)$

$A = 250$ sq ft

Area of Pool

$A = \pi r^2$

$A = \pi(10)^2$

$A = 314.159$ sq. ft.

Area of Garden

$A = s^2$

$A = (20)^2$

$A = 400$ sq. ft.

Total area to fertilize = Lot area - (House + Driveway + Pool + Garden)

$$= 17,000 - (4,000 + 250 + 314.159 + 400)$$
$$= 12,035.841 \text{ sq ft}$$

Number of bags needed = Total area to fertilize / 4,500 sq.ft. bag

$$= 12,035.841 / 4,500$$
$$= 2.67 \text{ bags}$$

Since we cannot purchase 2.67 bags we must purchase 3 full bags.

Total cost = Number of bags * $7.95
$$= 3 * \$7.95$$
$$= \$23.85$$

Examining the change in area or volume of a given figure requires first to find the existing area given the original dimensions and then finding the new area given the increased dimensions.

Sample problem:

Given the rectangle below determine the change in area if the length is increased by 5 and the width is increased by 7.

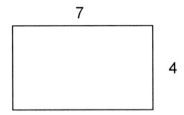

7

4

Draw and label a sketch of the new rectangle.

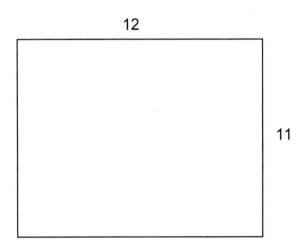

12

11

Find the areas.

Area of original = LW
    = (7)(4)
    = 28 units^2

Area of enlarged shape = LW
    = (12)(11)
    = 132 units^2

The change in area is 132 − 28 = 104 units^2.

It is necessary to be familiar with the metric and customary system in order to estimate measurements.

Some common equivalents include:

ITEM	APPROXIMATELY EQUAL TO	
	METRIC	IMPERIAL
large paper clip	1 gram	1 ounce
1 quart	1 liter	
average sized man	75 kilograms	170 pounds
1 yard	1 meter	
math textbook	1 kilogram	2 pounds
1 mile	1 kilometer	
1 foot	30 centimeters	
thickness of a dime	1 millimeter	0.1 inches

Estimate the measurement of the following items:

The length of an adult cow = _____ meters
The thickness of a compact disc = _____ millimeters
Your height = _____ meters
length of your nose = _____ centimeters
weight of your math textbook = _____ kilograms
weight of an automobile = _____ kilograms
weight of an aspirin = _____ grams

Given a set of objects and their measurements, the use of rounding procedures is helpful when attempting to round to the nearest given unit.

When rounding to a given place value, it is necessary to look at the number in the next smaller place. If this number is 5 or more, the number in the place we are rounding to is increased by one and all numbers to the right are changed to zero. If the number is less than 5, the number in the place we are rounding to stays the same and all numbers to the right are changed to zero.

One method of rounding measurements can require an additional step. First, the measurement must be converted to a decimal number. Then the rules for rounding applied.

Sample problem:

1. Round the measurements to the given units.

MEASUREMENT	ROUND TO NEAREST	ANSWER
1 foot 7 inches	foot	2 ft
5 pound 6 ounces	pound	5 pounds
5 9/16 inches	inch	6 inches

Solution:

Convert each measurement to a decimal number. Then apply the rules for rounding.

$$1 \text{ foot 7 inches} = 1\frac{7}{12} \text{ ft} = 1.58333 \text{ ft, round up to 2 ft}$$

$$5 \text{ pounds 6 ounces} = 5\frac{6}{16} \text{ pounds} = 5.375 \text{ pound, round to 5 pounds}$$

$$5\frac{9}{16} \text{ inches} = 5.5625 \text{ inches, round up to 6 inches}$$

There are many methods for converting measurements within a system. One method is to multiply the given measurement by a conversion factor. This conversion factor is the ratio of:

$$\frac{\text{new units}}{\text{old units}} \quad \text{OR} \quad \frac{\text{what you want}}{\text{what you have}}$$

Sample problems:

1. Convert 3 miles to yards.

$$\frac{3 \text{ miles}}{1} \times \frac{1,760 \text{ yards}}{1 \text{ mile}} = \frac{\text{yards}}{}$$

$$= 5,280 \text{ yards}$$

1. multiply by the conversion factor
2. cancel the miles units
3. solve

2. Convert 8,750 meters to kilometers.

$$\frac{8{,}750 \text{ meters}}{1} \times \frac{1 \text{ kilometer}}{1000 \text{ meters}} = \frac{\text{km}}{}$$

1. multiply by the conversion factor
2. cancel the meters units
3. solve

$$= 8.75 \text{ kilometers}$$

Use the formulas to find the volume and surface area.

FIGURE	VOLUME	TOTAL SURFACE AREA
Right Cylinder	$\pi r^2 h$	$2\pi rh + 2\pi r^2$
Right Cone	$\dfrac{\pi r^2 h}{3}$	$\pi r\sqrt{r^2 + h^2} + \pi r^2$
Sphere	$\dfrac{4}{3}\pi r^3$	$4\pi r^2$
Rectangular Solid	LWH	$2LW + 2WH + 2LH$

Note: $\sqrt{r^2 + h^2}$ is equal to the slant height of the cone.

Sample problem:

1. Given the figure below, find the volume and surface area.

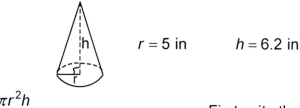

$r = 5$ in $h = 6.2$ in

Volume $= \dfrac{\pi r^2 h}{3}$ First write the formula.

$\dfrac{1}{3}\pi(5^2)(6.2)$ Then substitute.

162.31562 cubic inches   Finally solve the problem.

Surface area $= \pi r\sqrt{r^2 + h^2} + \pi r^2$ First write the formula.

$\pi 5\sqrt{5^2 + 6.2^2} + \pi 5^2$ Then substitute.
203.6 square inches   Compute.

Note: volume is always given in cubic units and area is always given in square units.

FIGURE	AREA FORMULA	PERIMETER FORMULA
Rectangle	LW	$2(L+W)$
Triangle	$\frac{1}{2}bh$	$a+b+c$
Parallelogram	bh	sum of lengths of sides
Trapezoid	$\frac{1}{2}h(a+b)$	sum of lengths of sides

Sample problems:

1. Find the area and perimeter of a rectangle if its length is 12 inches and its diagonal is 15 inches.

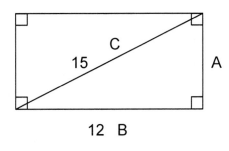

1. Draw and label sketch.
2. Since the height is still needed use Pythagorean formula to find missing leg of the triangle.

$$A^2 + B^2 = C^2$$
$$A^2 + 12^2 = 15^2$$
$$A^2 = 15^2 - 12^2$$
$$A^2 = 81$$
$$A = 9$$

Now use this information to find the area and perimeter.

$A = LW$	$P = 2(L+W)$	1. write formula
$A = (12)(9)$	$P = 2(12+9)$	2. substitute
$A = 108\ \text{in}^2$	$P = 42$ inches	3. solve

Given a circular figure the formulas are as follows:

$$A = \pi r^2 \qquad\qquad C = \pi d \quad \text{or} \quad 2\pi r$$

Sample problem:

1. If the area of a circle is 50 cm^2, find the circumference.

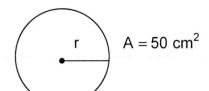

$A = 50\ \text{cm}^2$

1. Draw sketch.

2. Determine what is still needed.

Use the area formula to find the radius.

$A = \pi r^2$ 1. write formula

$50 = \pi r^2$ 2. substitute

$\dfrac{50}{\pi} = r^2$ 3. divide by π

$15.915 = r^2$ 4. substitute

$\sqrt{15.915} = \sqrt{r^2}$ 5. take square root of both sides

$3.989 \approx r$ 6. compute

Use the approximate answer (due to rounding) to find the circumference.

$C = 2\pi r$ 1. write formula

$C = 2\pi \, (3.989)$ 2. substitute

$C \approx 25.064$ 3. compute

Use appropriate problem solving strategies to find the solution.

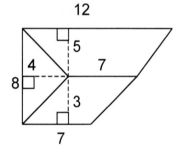

1. Find the area of the given figure.

2. Cut the figure into familiar shapes.

3. Identify what type figures are given and write the appropriate formulas.

Area of figure 1 (triangle)	Area of figure 2 (parallelogram)	Area of figure 3 (trapezoid)
$A = \dfrac{1}{2}bh$	$A = bh$	$A = \dfrac{1}{2}h(a+b)$
$A = \dfrac{1}{2}(8)(4)$	$A = (7)(3)$	$A = \dfrac{1}{2}(5)(12+7)$
$A = 16$ sq. ft	$A = 21$ sq. ft	$A = 47.5$ sq. ft

Now find the total area by adding the area of all figures.

Total area $= 16 + 21 + 47.5$
Total area $= 84.5$ square ft

FIGURE	LATERAL AREA	TOTAL AREA	VOLUME
Right prism	Ph	2B+Ph	Bh
Regular Pyramid	1/2Pl	1/2Pl+B	1/3Bh

P = Perimeter
h = height
B = Area of Base
l = slant height

Find the total area of the given figure:

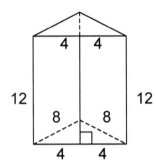

1. Since this is a triangular prism, first find the area of the bases.

2. Find the area of each rectangular lateral face.

3. Add the areas together.

$A = \frac{1}{2}bh$ $A = LW$ 1. write formula

$8^2 = 4^2 + h^2$ 2. find the height of
$h = 6.928$ the base triangle

$A = \frac{1}{2}(8)(6.928)$ $A = (8)(12)$ 3. substitute known values

$A = 27.713$ sq. units $A = 96$ sq. units   4. compute

Total Area $= 2(27.713) + 3(96)$
$\qquad\quad = 343.426$ sq. units

FIGURE	VOLUME	TOTAL SURFACE AREA	LATERAL AREA
Right Cylinder	$\pi r^2 h$	$2\pi rh + 2\pi r^2$	$2\pi rh$
Right Cone	$\dfrac{\pi r^2 h}{3}$	$\pi r\sqrt{r^2 + h^2} + \pi r^2$	$\pi r\sqrt{r^2 + h^2}$

Note: $\sqrt{r^2 + h^2}$ is equal to the slant height of the cone.

Sample problem:

1. A water company is trying to decide whether to use traditional cylindrical paper cups or to offer conical paper cups since both cost the same. The traditional cups are 8 cm wide and 14 cm high. The conical cups are 12 cm wide and 19 cm high. The company will use the cup that holds the most water.

Draw and label a sketch of each.

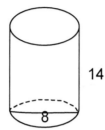
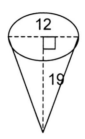

$V = \pi r^2 h$ $V = \dfrac{\pi r^2 h}{3}$ 1. write formula

$V = \pi (4)^2 (14)$ $V = \dfrac{1}{3} \pi (6)^2 (19)$ 2. substitute

$V = 703.717 \text{ cm}^3$ $V = 716.283 \text{ cm}^3$ 3. solve

The choice should be the conical cup since its volume is more.

FIGURE	VOLUME	TOTAL SURFACE AREA
Sphere	$\dfrac{4}{3}\pi r^3$	$4\pi r^2$

Sample problem:

1. How much material is needed to make a basketball that has a diameter of 15 inches? How much air is needed to fill the basketball?

Draw and label a sketch:

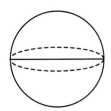

D=15 inches

Total surface area   Volume

$TSA = 4\pi r^2$ $V = \dfrac{4}{3}\pi r^3$ 1. write formula

$= 4\pi(7.5)^2$ $= \dfrac{4}{3}\pi(7.5)^3$ 2. substitute

$= 706.9 \text{ in}^2$ $= 1767.1 \text{ in}^3$ 3. solve

Competency 0011   Understand the principles and properties of Euclidean geometry in two and three dimensions.

The converse of the Pythagorean Theorem states that if the square of one side of a triangle is equal to the sum of the squares of the other two sides, then the triangle is a right triangle.

Example:
Given $\triangle XYZ$, with sides measuring 12, 16 and 20 cm. Is this a right triangle?

$$c^2 = a^2 + b^2$$
$$20^2 \ ? \ 12^2 + 16^2$$
$$400 \ ? \ 144 + 256$$
$$400 \ = 400$$

Yes, the triangle is a right triangle.

This theorem can be expanded to determine if triangles are obtuse or acute.

If the square of the longest side of a triangle is greater than the sum of the squares of the other two sides, then the triangle is an obtuse triangle.
and
If the square of the longest side of a triangle is less than the sum of the squares of the other two sides, then the triangle is an acute triangle.

Example:
Given $\triangle LMN$ with sides measuring 7, 12, and 14 inches. Is the triangle right, acute, or obtuse?

$$14^2 \ ? \ 7^2 + 12^2$$
$$196 \ ? \ 49 + 144$$
$$196 > 193$$

Therefore, the triangle is obtuse.

Every angle has exactly one ray which bisects the angle. If a point on such a bisector is located, then the point is equidistant from the two sides of the angle. Distance from a point to a side is measured along a segment which is perpendicular to the angle's side. The converse is also true. If a point is equidistant from the sides of an angle, then the point is on the bisector of the angle.

Every segment has exactly one line which is both perpendicular to and bisects the segment. If a point on such a perpendicular bisector is located, then the point is equidistant to the endpoints of the segment. The converse is also true. If a point is equidistant from the endpoints of a segments, then that point is on the perpendicular bisector of the segment.

If three or more segments intersect in a single point, the point is called a point of concurrency.

The following sets of special segments all intersect in points of concurrency.

1. Angle Bisectors
2. Medians
3. Altitudes
4. Perpendicular Bisectors

The points of concurrency can lie inside the triangle, outside the triangle, or on one of the sides of the triangle. The following table summarizes this information.

Possible Location(s) of the
Points of Concurrency

	Inside the Triangle	Outside the Triangle	On the Triangle
Angle Bisectors	x		
Medians	x		
Altitudes	x	x	x
Perpendicular Bisectors	x	x	x

In geometry, the point, line, and plane are key concepts and can be discussed in relation to each other.

collinear points
are all on the same line

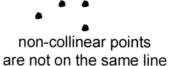

non-collinear points
are not on the same line

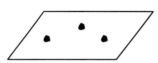

coplanar points
are on the same plane

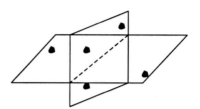

non-coplanar points
are not on the same plane

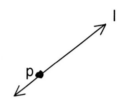

Point p is in line l
Point p is on line l
l contains P
l passes through P

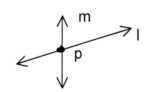

l and m intersect
at p
p is the intersection
of l and m

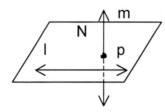

l and p are in plane N
N contains p and l
m intersects N at p
p is the intersection
of m and N

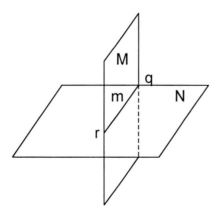

Planes M and N intersect at rq
rq is the intersection
of M and N
rq is in M and N
M and N contain rq

The classifying of angles refers to the angle measure. The naming of angles refers to the letters or numbers used to label the angle.

Sample Problem:

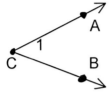

$\overrightarrow{CA}$ (read ray CA) and $\overrightarrow{CB}$ are the sides of the angle.
The angle can be called $\angle ACB$, $\angle BCA$, $\angle C$ or $\angle 1$.

Angles are classified according to their size as follows:

acute: greater than 0 and less than 90 degrees
right: exactly 90 degrees
obtuse: greater than 90 and less than 180 degrees
straight: exactly 180 degrees

Angles can be classified in a number of ways. Some of those classifications are outlined here.

Adjacent angles have a common vertex and one common side but no interior points in common.

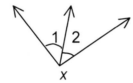

⁕ Complementary angles add up to 90 degrees.

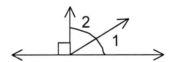

⁕ Supplementary angles add up to 180 degrees.

⁕ Vertical angles have sides that form two pairs of opposite rays.

⁕ Corresponding angles are in the same corresponding position on two parallel lines cut by a transversal.

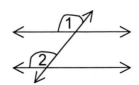

Alternate interior angles are diagonal angles on the inside of two parallel lines cut by a transversal.

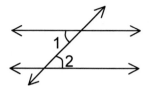

Alternate exterior angles are diagonal angles on the outside of two parallel lines cut by a transversal.

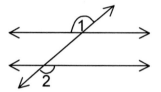

Parallel lines or planes do not intersect.

Perpendicular lines or planes form a 90-degree angle to each other.

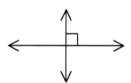

Intersecting lines share a common point and intersecting planes share a common set of points or line.

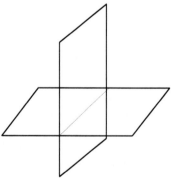

Skew lines do not intersect and do not lie on the same plane.

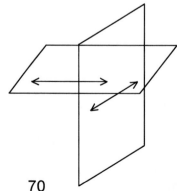

A **triangle** is a polygon with three sides.

Triangles can be classified by the types of angles or the lengths of their sides.

Classifying by angles:

An **acute** triangle has exactly three *acute* angles.
A **right** triangle has one *right* angle.
An **obtuse** triangle has one *obtuse* angle.

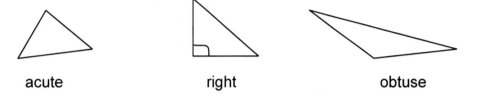

acute   right   obtuse

Classifying by sides:

All *three* sides of an **equilateral** triangle are the same length.
Two sides of an **isosceles** triangle are the same length.
None of the sides of a **scalene** triangle is the same length.

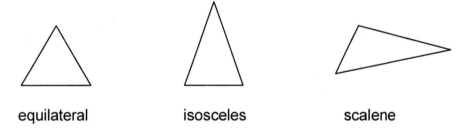

equilateral   isosceles   scalene

The sum of the measures of the angles of a triangle is 180°.

Example 1:
Can a triangle have two right angles?
No. A right angle measures 90°, therefore the sum of two right angles would be 180° and there could not be third angle.

Example 2:
Can a triangle have two obtuse angles?
No. Since an obtuse angle measures more than 90° the sum of two obtuse angles would be greater than 180°.

Example 3:
Can a right triangle be obtuse?
No. Once again, the sum of the angles would be more than 180°.

Example 4:

In a triangle, the measure of the second angle is three times the first. The third angle equals the sum of the measures of the first two angles. Find the number of degrees in each angle.

Let x = the number of degrees in the first angle
$3x$ = the number of degrees in the second angle
$x + 3x$ = the measure of the third angle

Since the sum of the measures of all three angles is 180°.

$$x + 3x + (x + 3x) = 180$$
$$8x = 180$$
$$x = 22.5$$
$$3x = 67.5$$
$$x + 3x = 90$$

Thus the angles measure 22.5°, 67.5°, and 90°. Additionally, the triangle is a right triangle.

EXTERIOR ANGLES

Two adjacent angles form a linear pair when they have a common side and their remaining sides form a straight angle. Angles in a linear pair are supplementary. An exterior angle of a triangle forms a linear pair with an angle of the triangle.

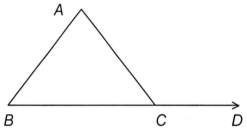

$\angle ACD$ is an exterior angle of triangle ABC, forming a linear pair with $\angle ACB$.

The measure of an exterior angle of a triangle is equal to the sum of the measures of the two non-adjacent interior angles.

Example:

In triangle ABC, the measure of $\angle A$ is twice the measure of $\angle B$. $\angle C$ is $30°$ more than their sum. Find the measure of the exterior angle formed at $\angle C$.

$$\text{Let} \quad x = \text{the measure of } \angle B$$
$$2x = \text{the measure of } \angle A$$
$$x + 2x + 30 = \text{the measure of } \angle C$$
$$x + 2x + x + 2x + 30 = 180$$
$$6x + 30 = 180$$
$$6x = 150$$
$$x = 25$$
$$2x = 50$$

It is not necessary to find the measure of the third angle, since the exterior angle equals the sum of the opposite interior angles. Thus the exterior angle at $\angle C$ measures $75°$.

A **polygon** is a simple closed figure composed of line segments. In a **regular polygon,** all sides are the same length and all angles are the same measure.

The sum of the measures of the **interior angles** of a polygon can be determined using the following formula, where n represents the number of angles in the polygon.

$$\text{Sum of } \angle s = 180(n - 2)$$

The measure of each angle of a regular polygon can be found by dividing the sum of the measures by the number of angles.

$$\text{Measure of } \angle = \frac{180(n - 2)}{n}$$

Example: Find the measure of each angle of a regular octagon.

Since an octagon has eight sides, each angle equals:

$$\frac{180(8 - 2)}{8} = \frac{180(6)}{8} = 135°$$

The sum of the measures of the **exterior angles** of a polygon, taken one angle at each vertex, equals $360°$.

The measure of each exterior angle of a regular polygon can be determined using the following formula, where n represents the number of angles in the polygon.

Measure of exterior $\angle$ of regular polygon = $180 - \dfrac{180(n-2)}{n}$

or, more simply $= \dfrac{360}{n}$

<u>Example</u>: Find the measure of the interior and exterior angles of a regular pentagon.

Since a pentagon has five sides, each exterior angle measures:

$\dfrac{360}{5} = 72°$

Since each exterior angle is supplementary to its interior angle, the interior angle measures $180 - 72$ or $108°$.

Congruent figures have the same size and shape. If one is placed above the other, it will fit exactly. Congruent lines have the same length. Congruent angles have equal measures.

The symbol for congruent is $\cong$.

Polygons (pentagons) *ABCDE* and *VWXYZ* are congruent. They are exactly the same size and shape.

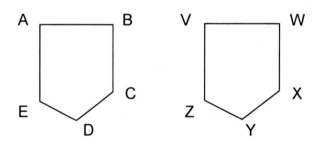

$ABCDE \cong VWXYZ$

Corresponding parts are those congruent angles and congruent sides, that is:

corresponding angles	corresponding sides
$\angle A \leftrightarrow \angle V$	$AB \leftrightarrow VW$
$\angle B \leftrightarrow \angle W$	$BC \leftrightarrow WX$
$\angle C \leftrightarrow \angle X$	$CD \leftrightarrow XY$
$\angle D \leftrightarrow \angle Y$	$DE \leftrightarrow YZ$
$\angle E \leftrightarrow \angle Z$	$AE \leftrightarrow VZ$

Two triangles can be proven congruent by comparing pairs of appropriate congruent corresponding parts.

SSS POSTULATE

If three sides of one triangle are congruent to three sides of another triangle, then the two triangles are congruent.

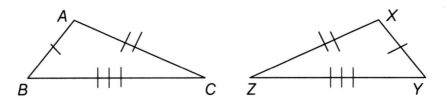

Since $AB \cong XY$, $BC \cong YZ$ and $AC \cong XZ$, then $\triangle ABC \cong \triangle XYZ$.

<u>Example</u>: Given isosceles triangle ABC with D the midpoint of base AC, prove the two triangles formed by AD are congruent.

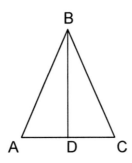

Proof:
1. Isosceles triangle ABC, D midpoint of base AC Given
2. $AB \cong BC$ An isosceles $\triangle$ has two congruent sides
3. $AD \cong DC$ Midpoint divides a line into two equal parts
4. $BD \cong BD$ Reflexive
5. $\triangle ABD \cong \triangle BCD$ SSS

SAS POSTULATE

If two sides and the included angle of one triangle are congruent to two sides and the included angle of another triangle, then the two triangles are congruent.

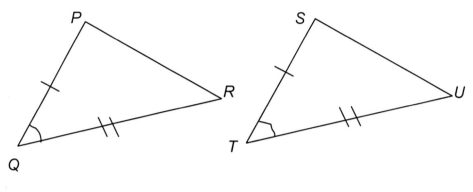

Example:

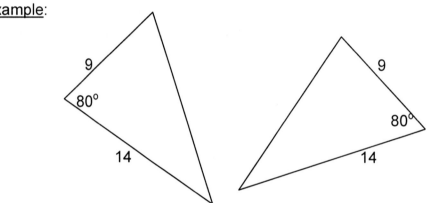

The two triangles are congruent by SAS.

ASA POSTULATE

If two angles and the included side of one triangle are congruent to two angles and the included side of another triangle, the triangles are congruent.

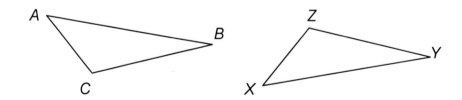

$\angle A \cong \angle X$, $\angle B \cong \angle Y$, $AB \cong XY$ then $\triangle ABC \cong \triangle XYZ$ by ASA

<u>Example:</u> Given two right triangles with one leg of each measuring 6 cm and the adjacent angle 37°, prove the triangles are congruent.

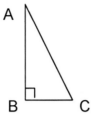
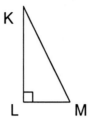

1. Right triangles *ABC* and *KLM*   Given
    AB = *KL* = 6 cm
    ∠*A* = ∠*K* = 37°

2. *AB* ≅ *KL*   Figures with the same
    ∠*A* ≅ ∠*K*   measure are congruent

3. ∠*B* ≅ ∠*L*   All right angles are
                                             congruent.

4. △*ABC* ≅ △ *KLM*   ASA

<u>Example:</u>
What method would you use to prove the triangles congruent?

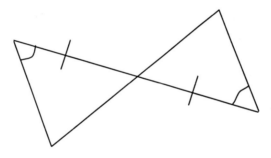

ASA because vertical angles are congruent.

AAS THEOREM

If two angles and a non-included side of one triangle are congruent to the corresponding parts of another triangle, then the triangles are congruent.

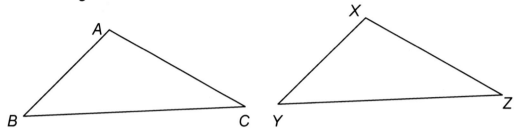

$\angle B \cong \angle Y$, $\angle C \cong \angle Z$, $AC \cong XZ$, then $\triangle ABC \cong \triangle XYZ$ by AAS.

We can derive this theorem because if two angles of the triangles are congruent, then the third angle must also be congruent. Therefore, we can use the ASA postulate.

HL THEOREM

If the hypotenuse and a leg of one right triangle are congruent to the corresponding parts of another right triangle, the triangles are congruent.

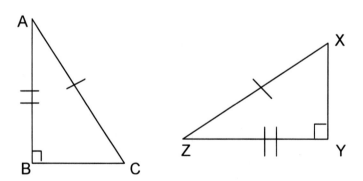

Since $\angle B$ and $\angle Y$ are right angles and $AC \cong XZ$ (hypotenuse of each triangle), $AB \cong YZ$ (corresponding leg of each triangle), then $\triangle ABC \cong \triangle XYZ$ by HL.

<u>Example</u>: What method would you use to prove the triangles congruent?

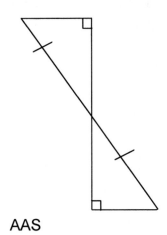

AAS

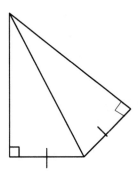

HL

Two figures that have the **same shape** are **similar**. Two polygons are similar if corresponding angles are congruent and corresponding sides are in proportion. Corresponding parts of similar polygons are proportional.

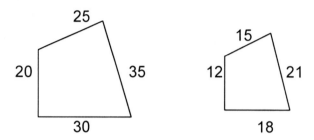

SIMILAR TRIANGLES

AA Similarity Postulate
If two angles of one triangle are congruent to two angles of another triangle, then the triangles are similar.

SAS Similarity Theorem
If an angle of one triangle is congruent to an angle of another triangle and the sides adjacent to those angles are in proportion, then the triangles are similar.

SSS Similarity Theorem
If the sides of two triangles are in proportion, then the triangles are similar.

Example:

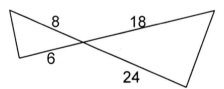

The two triangles are similar since the sides are proportional and the vertical angles are congruent.

<u>Example</u>: Given two similar quadrilaterals. Find the lengths of sides *x, y,* and *z.*

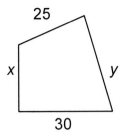

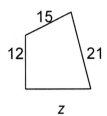

Since corresponding sides are proportional:

$$\frac{15}{25} = \frac{3}{5} \text{ so the scale is } \frac{3}{5}$$

$$\frac{12}{x} = \frac{3}{5} \qquad\qquad \frac{21}{y} = \frac{3}{5} \qquad\qquad \frac{z}{30} = \frac{3}{5}$$

$$3x = 60 \qquad\qquad 3y = 105 \qquad\qquad 5z = 90$$
$$x = 20 \qquad\qquad y = 35 \qquad\qquad z = 18$$

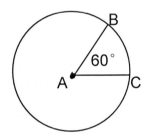

Central angle BAC $= 60°$

Minor arc BC $= 60°$

Major arc BC $= 360 - 60 = 300°$

If you draw **two radii** in a circle, the angle they form with the center as the vertex is a central angle. The piece of the circle "inside" the angle is an arc. Just like a central angle, an arc can have any degree measure from 0 to 360. The measure of an arc is equal to the measure of the central angle which forms the arc. Since a diameter forms a semicircle and the measure of a straight angle like a diameter is 180°, the measure of a semicircle is also 180°.

Given two points on a circle, there are two different arcs which the two points form. Except in the case of semicircles, one of the two arcs will always be greater than 180° and the other will be less than 180°. The arc less than 180° is a minor arc and the arc greater than 180° is a major arc.

Examples:

1.

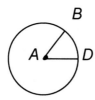

$m\angle BAD = 45°$
What is the measure of the major arc *BD*?

$\angle BAD = $ minor arc *BD*

$45° = $ minor arc *BD*

The measure of the central angle is the same as the measure of the arc it forms.

$360 - 45 = $ major arc *BD*

$315° = $ major arc *BD*

A major and minor arc always add to $360°$.

2.

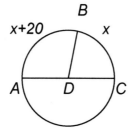

$\overline{AC}$ is a diameter of circle *D*. What is the measure of $\angle BDC$?

$m\angle ADB + m\angle BDC = 180°$

$x + 20 + x = 180$

$2x + 20 = 180$

$2x = 160$

$x = 80$

A diameter forms a semicircle which has a measure of $180°$.

minor arc $BC = 80°$

$m\angle BDC = 80°$

A central angle has the same measure as the arc it forms.

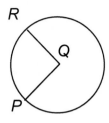

$$\frac{\angle PQR}{360°} = \frac{\text{length of arc } RP}{\text{circumference of } \odot Q} = \frac{\text{area of sector } PQR}{\text{area of } \odot Q}$$

While an arc has a measure associated to the degree measure of a central angle, it also has a length which is a fraction of the circumference of the circle.

For each central angle and its associated arc, there is a sector of the circle which resembles a pie piece. The area of such a sector is a fraction of the area of the circle.

The fractions used for the area of a sector and length of its associated arc are both equal to the ratio of the central angle to 360°.

Examples:

1.

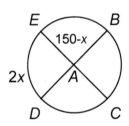

$\odot A$ has a radius of 4 cm. What is the length of arc *ED*?

$2x + 150 - x = 180$

$x + 150 = 180$

$x = 30$ Arc *BE* and arc *DE* make a semicircle.

Arc $ED = 2(30) = 60°$ The ratio 60° to 360° is equal to the ratio of arch length *ED* to the circumference of $\odot A$

$\frac{60}{360} = \frac{\text{arc length } ED}{2\pi 4}$

$\frac{1}{6} = \frac{\text{arc length}}{8\pi}$ Cross multiply and solve for the arc length.

$\frac{8\pi}{6} = \text{arc length}$

arc length $ED = \dfrac{4\pi}{3}$ cm.

2.

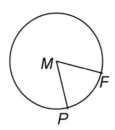

The radius of ⊙ M is 3 cm. The length of arc *PF* is 2π cm. What is the area of sector *PMF*?

Circumference of ⊙ $M = 2\pi(3) = 6\pi$

Find the circumference and area of the circle.

Area of ⊙ $M = \pi(3)^2 = 9\pi$

$$\frac{\text{area of } MPF}{9\pi} = \frac{2\pi}{6\pi}$$

The ratio of the sector area to the circle area is the same as the arc length to the circumference.

$$\frac{\text{area of } MPF}{9\pi} = \frac{1}{3}$$

$$\text{area of } MPF = \frac{9\pi}{3}$$

$$\text{area of } MPF = 3\pi$$

Solve for the area of the sector.

A **tangent line** intersects a circle in exactly one point. If a radius is drawn to that point, the radius will be perpendicular to the tangent.

A **chord** is a segment with endpoints on the circle. If a radius or diameter is perpendicular to a chord, the radius will cut the chord into two equal parts.

If **two chords** in the same circle have the same length, the two chords will have arcs that are the same length, and the two chords will be equidistant from the center of the circle. Distance from the center to a chord is measured by finding the length of a segment from the center perpendicular to the chord.

Examples:

1.

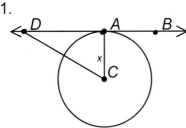

$\overline{DB}$ is tangent to $\angle C$ at A.
$m\angle ADC = 40°$ Find x.

$\overline{AC} \perp \overline{DB}$

A radius is $\perp$ to a tangent at the point of tangency.

$m\angle DAC = 90°$

Two segments that are $\perp$ form a $90°$ angle.

$40 + 90 + x = 180$

The sum of the angles of a triangle is $180°$.

$x = 50°$

Solve for x.

2.

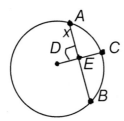

$\overline{CD}$ is a radius and $\overline{CD} \perp$ chord $\overline{AB}$.
$AB = 10$. Find x.

$x = \dfrac{1}{2}(10)$

$x = 5$

If a radius is $\perp$ to a chord, the radius bisects the chord.

Angles with their vertices on the circle:

An inscribed angle is an angle whose vertex is on the circle. Such an angle could be formed by two chords, two diameters, two secants, or a secant and a tangent. An inscribed angle has one arc of the circle in its interior.

The measure of the inscribed angle is one-half the measure of this intercepted arc. If two inscribed angles intercept the same arc, the two angles are congruent (i.e. their measures are equal). If an inscribed angle intercepts an entire semicircle, the angle is a right angle.

Angles with their vertices in a circle's interior:

When two chords intersect inside a circle, two sets of vertical angles are formed. Each set of vertical angles intercepts two arcs which are across from each other. The measure of an angle formed by two chords in a circle is equal to one-half the sum of the angle intercepted by the angle and the arc intercepted by its vertical angle.

Angles with their vertices in a circle's exterior:

If an angle has its vertex outside of the circle and each side of the circle intersects the circle, then the angle contains two different arcs. The measure of the angle is equal to one-half the difference of the two arcs.

Examples:

1.

Find x and y.
arc $DC = 40°$

$$m\angle DAC = \frac{1}{2}(40) = 20°$$

$\angle DAC$ and $\angle DBC$ are both inscribed angles, so each one has a measure equal to one-half the measure of arc DC.

$$m\angle DBC = \frac{1}{2}(40) = 20°$$

$x = 20°$ and $y = 20°$

Intersecting chords:

If two chords intersect inside a circle, each chord is divided into two smaller segments. The product of the lengths of the two segments formed from one chord equals the product of the lengths of the two segments formed from the other chord.

Intersecting tangent segments:

If two tangent segments intersect outside of a circle, the two segments have the same length.

Intersecting secant segments:

If two secant segments intersect outside a circle, a portion of each segment will lie inside the circle and a portion (called the exterior segment) will lie outside the circle. The product of the length of one secant segment and the length of its exterior segment equals the product of the length of the other secant segment and the length of its exterior segment.

Tangent segments intersecting secant segments:

If a tangent segment and a secant segment intersect outside a circle, the square of the length of the tangent segment equals the product of the length of the secant segment and its exterior segment.

Examples:

1.

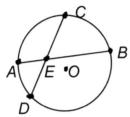

$\overline{AB}$ and $\overline{CD}$ are chords.
$CE=10$, $ED=x$, $AE=5$, $EB=4$

$$(AE)(EB) = (CE)(ED)$$

Since the chords intersect in the circle, the products of the segment pieces are equal.

$$5(4) = 10x$$
$$20 = 10x$$
$$x = 2$$

Solve for x.

2.

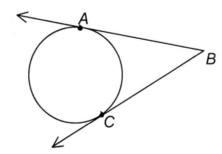

$\overline{AB}$ and $\overline{CD}$ are chords.
$\overline{AB} = x^2 + x - 2$
$\overline{BC} = x^2 - 3x + 5$
Find the length of
$\overline{AB}$ and $\overline{BC}$.

$$\overline{AB} = x^2 + x - 2$$
$$\overline{BC} = x^2 - 3x + 5$$

Given

$$\overline{AB} = \overline{BC}$$

Intersecting tangents are equal.

$$x^2 + x - 2 = x^2 - 3x + 5$$

Set the expression equal and solve.

$$4x = 7$$

$$x = 1.75$$

Substitute and solve.

$$(1.75)^2 + 1.75 - 2 = \overline{AB}$$

$$\overline{AB} = \overline{BC} = 2.81$$

$$(1.75)^2 + 1.75 - 2 = \overline{AB}$$

$$\overline{AB} = \overline{BC} = 2.81$$

Given the figure below, find the area by dividing the polygon into smaller shapes.

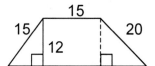

1. divide the figure into two triangles and a rectangle.

2. find the missing lengths.

3. find the area of each part.

4. find the sum of all areas.

Find base of both right triangles using Pythagorean Formula:

$$a^2 + b^2 = c^2$$
$$a^2 + 12^2 = 15^2$$
$$a^2 = 225 - 144$$
$$a^2 = 81$$
$$a = 9$$

$$a^2 + b^2 = c^2$$
$$a^2 + 12^2 = 20^2$$
$$a^2 = 400 - 144$$
$$a^2 = 256$$
$$a = 16$$

Area of triangle 1	Area of triangle 2	Area of rectangle
$A = \dfrac{1}{2}bh$	$A = \dfrac{1}{2}bh$	$A = LW$
$A = \dfrac{1}{2}(9)(12)$	$A = \dfrac{1}{2}(16)(12)$	$A = (15)(12)$
$A = 54$ sq. units	$A = 96$ sq. units	$A = 180$ sq. units

Find the sum of all three figures.

$$54 + 96 + 180 = 330 \text{ square units}$$

Polygons are similar if and only if there is a one-to-one correspondence between their vertices such that the corresponding angles are congruent and the lengths of corresponding sides are proportional.

Given the rectangles below, compare the area and perimeter.

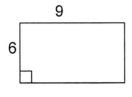
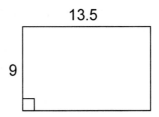

$A = LW$	$A = LW$	1. write formula
$A = (6)(9)$	$A = (9)(13.5)$	2. substitute known values
$A = 54$ sq. units	$A = 121.5$ sq. units	3. compute
$P = 2(L + W)$	$P = 2(L + W)$	1. write formula
$P = 2(6 + 9)$	$P = 2(9 + 13.5)$	2. substitute known values
$P = 30$ units	$P = 45$ units	3. compute

Notice that the areas relate to each other in the following manner:

Ratio of sides $9/13.5 = 2/3$

Multiply the first area by the square of the reciprocal $(3/2)^2$ to get the second area.
$$54 \times (3/2)^2 = 121.5$$

The perimeters relate to each other in the following manner:

Ratio of sides $9/13.5 = 2/3$

Multiply the perimeter of the first by the reciprocal of the ratio to get the perimeter of the second.
$$30 \times 3/2 = 45$$

Competency 0012   Understand the principles and properties of coordinate and transformational geometries.

In order to accomplish the task of finding the distance from a given point to another given line the perpendicular line that intersects the point and line must be drawn and the equation of the other line written. From this information the point of intersection can be found. This point and the original point are used in the distance formula given below:

$$D = \sqrt{(x_2 - x_1)^2 + (y_2 - y_1)^2}$$

Sample Problem:

1. Given the point ($^-4$,3) and the line $y = 4x + 2$, find the distance from the point to the line.

$y = 4x + 2$	1. Find the slope of the given line by solving for y.
$y = 4x + 2$	2. The slope is 4/1, the perpendicular line will have a slope of $^-1/4$.
$y = \left(^-1/4\right)x + b$	3. Use the new slope and the given point to find the equation of the perpendicular line.
$3 = \left(^-1/4\right)\left(^-4\right) + b$	4. Substitute ($^-4$,3) into the equation.
$3 = 1 + b$	5. Solve.
$2 = b$	6. Given the value for b, write the equation of the perpendicular line.
$y = \left(^-1/4\right)x + 2$	7. Write in standard form.
$x + 4y = 8$	8. Use both equations to solve by elimination to get the point of intersection.
$^-4x + y = 2$ $\underline{x + 4y = 8}$	9. Multiply the bottom row by 4.
$^-4x + y = 2$ $\underline{4x + 16y = 32}$ $17y = 34$ $y = 2$	10. Solve.
$y = 4x + 2$	11. Substitute to find the x value.
$2 = 4x + 2$ $x = 0$	12. Solve.

(0,2) is the point of intersection. Use this point on the original line and the original point to calculate the distance between them.

$$D = \sqrt{(x_2 - x_1)^2 + (y_2 - y_1)^2}$$ where points are (0,2) and (-4,3).

$$D = \sqrt{(^-4 - 0)^2 + (3 - 2)^2}$$ 1. Substitute.

$$D = \sqrt{(16) + (1)}$$ 2. Simplify.

$$D = \sqrt{17}$$

The distance between two parallel lines, such as line AB and line CD as shown below is the line segment RS, the perpendicular between the two parallels.

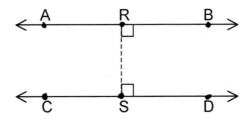

Sample Problem:

Given the geometric figure below, find the distance between the two parallel sides AB and CD.

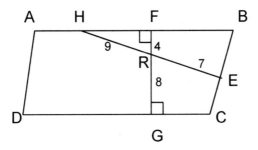

The distance FG is 12 units.

The key to applying the distance formula is to understand the problem before beginning.

$$D = \sqrt{(x_2 - x_1)^2 + (y_2 - y_1)^2}$$

Sample Problem:

1. Find the perimeter of a figure with vertices at (4, 5), (−4 , 6) and (−5,−8).

The figure being described is a triangle. Therefore, the distance for all three sides must be found. Carefully identify all three sides before beginning.

$$\text{Side } 1 = (4,5) \text{ to } (-4,6)$$
$$\text{Side } 2 = (-4,6) \text{ to } (-5,-8)$$
$$\text{Side } 3 = (-5,-8) \text{ to } (4,5)$$

$$D_1 = \sqrt{(-4-4)^2 + (6-5)^2} = \sqrt{65}$$

$$D_2 = \sqrt{((^-5-(^-4))^2 + (^-8-6)^2} = \sqrt{197}$$

$$D_3 = \sqrt{((4-(^-5))^2 + (5-(^-8)^2} = \sqrt{250} \text{ or } 5\sqrt{10} \text{ [SA17]}$$

$$\text{Perimeter} = \sqrt{65} + \sqrt{197} + 5\sqrt{10}$$

Midpoint Definition:

If a line segment has endpoints of (x_1, y_1) and (x_2, y_2), then the midpoint can be found using:

$$\left(\frac{x_1 + x_2}{2}, \frac{y_1 + y_2}{2} \right)$$

Sample problems:

1. Find the center of a circle with a diameter whose endpoints are $(3, 7)$ and $(-4, -5)$.

$$\text{Midpoint} = \left(\frac{3 + (-4)}{2}, \frac{7 + (-5)}{2} \right)$$

$$\text{Midpoint} = \left(\frac{-1}{2}, 1 \right)$$

2. Find the midpoint given the two points $\left(5, 8\sqrt{6} \right)$ and $\left(9, -4\sqrt{6} \right)$.

$$\text{Midpoint} = \left(\frac{5 + 9}{2}, \frac{8\sqrt{6} + (-4\sqrt{6})}{2} \right)$$

$$\text{Midpoint} = \left(7, 2\sqrt{6} \right)$$

We can represent any two-dimensional geometric figure in the **Cartesian** or **rectangular coordinate system**. The Cartesian or rectangular coordinate system is formed by two perpendicular axes (coordinate axes): the X-axis and the Y-axis. If we know the dimensions of a two-dimensional, or planar, figure, we can use this coordinate system to visualize the shape of the figure.

Example: Represent an isosceles triangle with two sides of length 4.

Draw the two sides along the x- and y- axes and connect the points (vertices).

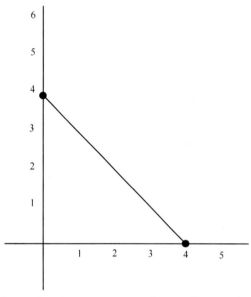

In order to represent three-dimensional figures, we need three coordinate axes (X, Y, and Z) which are all mutually perpendicular to each other. Since we cannot draw three mutually perpendicular axes on a two-dimensional surface, we use oblique representations.

Example: Represent a cube with sides of 2.

Once again, we draw three sides along the three axes to make things easier.

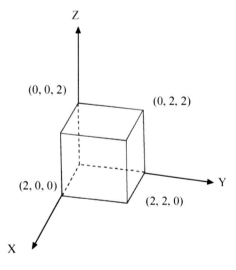

Each point has three coordinates (x, y, z).

A **transformation** is a change in the position, shape, or size of a geometric figure. **Transformational geometry** is the study of manipulating objects by flipping, twisting, turning and scaling. **Symmetry** is exact similarity between two parts or halves, as if one were a mirror image of the other.

There are four basic transformational symmetries that can be used in tessellations: **translation, rotation, reflection,** and **glide reflection**. The transformation of an object is called its image. If the original object was labeled with letters, such as $ABCD$, the image may be labeled with the same letters followed by a prime symbol, $A'B'C'D'$.

A **translation** is a transformation that "slides" an object a fixed distance in a given direction. The original object and its translation have the same shape and size, and they face in the same direction.

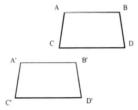

An example of a translation in architecture would be stadium seating. The seats are the same size and the same shape and face in the same direction.

A **rotation** is a transformation that turns a figure about a fixed point called the center of rotation. An object and its rotation are the same shape and size, but the figures may be turned in different directions. Rotations can occur in either a clockwise or a counterclockwise direction.

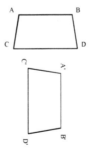

Rotations can be seen in wallpaper and art, and a Ferris wheel is an example of rotation.

An object and its **reflection** have the same shape and size, but the figures face in opposite directions.

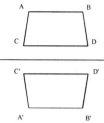

The line (where a mirror may be placed) is called the **line of reflection**. The distance from a point to the line of reflection is the same as the distance from the point's image to the line of reflection.

A **glide reflection** is a combination of a reflection and a translation.

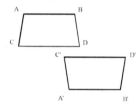

Another type of transformation is **dilation**. A dilation is a transformation that "shrinks" or "makes it bigger."

Example:

Using dilation to transform a diagram.

Starting with a triangle whose center of dilation is point P,

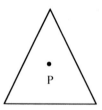

we dilate the lengths of the sides by the same factor to create a new triangle

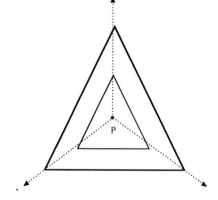

Competency 0013   Understand right triangle trigonometry and the conceptual foundations of calculus.

Given right triangle ABC, the adjacent side and opposite side can be identified for each angle A and B.

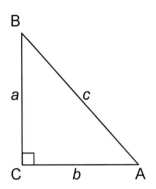

Looking at angle A, it can be determined that side *b* is adjacent to angle A and side *a* is opposite angle A.

If we now look at angle B, we see that side a is adjacent to angle B and side *b* is opposite angle B.

The longest side (opposite the 90-degree angle) is always called the hypotenuse.

The basic trigonometric ratios are listed below:

Sine = opposite   Cosine = adjacent   Tangent = opposite
      hypotenuse   hypotenuse   adjacent

Sample problem:

1. Use triangle ABC to find the sin, cos and tan for angle A.

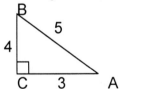

sinA = 4/5
cosA = 3/5
tanA = 4/3

Use the basic trigonometric ratios of sine, cosine, and tangent to solve for the missing sides of right triangles when given at least one of the acute angles.

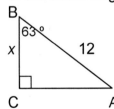

In the triangle ABC, an acute angle is 63 degrees and the length of the hypotenuse, 12. The missing side is the one adjacent to the given angle.

The appropriate trigonometric ratio to use would be cosine since we are looking for the adjacent side and we have the length of the hypotenuse.

$$\text{Cos} x = \frac{\text{adjacent}}{\text{Hypotenuse}}$$ 1. Write formula.

$$\text{Cos } 63 = \frac{x}{12}$$ 2. Substitute known values.

$$0.454 = \frac{x}{12}$$

$$x = 5.448$$ 3. Solve.

The **limit of a function** is the y value that the graph approaches as the x values approach a certain number. To find a limit there are two points to remember.

1. Factor the expression completely and cancel all common factors in fractions.
2. Substitute the number to which the variable is approaching. In most cases this produces the value of the limit.

If the variable in the limit is approaching ∞, factor and simplify first; then examine the result. If the result does not involve a fraction with the variable in the denominator, the limit is usually also equal to ∞. If the variable is in the denominator of the fraction, the denominator is getting larger which makes the entire fraction smaller. In other words the limit is zero.

Examples:

1. $\lim\limits_{x \to {}^{-}3} \dfrac{x^2 + 5x + 6}{x + 3} + 4x$ Factor the numerator.

$\lim\limits_{x \to {}^{-}3} \dfrac{(x+3)(x+2)}{(x+3)} + 4x$ Cancel the common factors.

$\lim\limits_{x \to {}^{-}3} (x + 2) + 4x$ Substitute $^{-}3$ for x.

$({}^{-}3 + 2) + 4({}^{-}3)$ Simplify.

$^{-}1 + {}^{-}12$

$^{-}13$

2. $\lim\limits_{x \to \infty} \dfrac{2x^2}{x^5}$ 　　　　Cancel the common factors.

$\lim\limits_{x \to \infty} \dfrac{2}{x^3}$

Since the denominator is getting larger, the entire fraction is getting smaller. The fraction is getting close to zero.

$\dfrac{2}{\infty^3}$

Practice problems:

1. $\lim\limits_{x \to \pi} 5x^2 + \sin x$　　　2. $\lim\limits_{x \to {}^-4} \dfrac{x^2 + 9x + 20}{x + 4}$

After simplifying an expression to evaluate a limit, substitute the value that the variable approaches. If the substitution results in either 0/0 or ∞/∞, use L'Hopital's rule to find the limit.

L'Hopital's rule states that you can find such limits by taking the derivative of the numerator and the derivative of the denominator, and then finding the limit of the resulting quotient.

Examples:

1. $\lim\limits_{x \to \infty} \dfrac{3x - 1}{x^2 + 2x + 3}$ 　　　No factoring is possible.

$\dfrac{3\infty - 1}{\infty^2 + 2\infty + 3}$ 　　　Substitute ∞ for x.

$\dfrac{\infty}{\infty}$

Since a constant times infinity is still a large number, $3(\infty) = \infty$.

$\lim\limits_{x \to \infty} \dfrac{3}{2x + 2}$

To find the limit, take the derivative of the numerator and denominator.

$\dfrac{3}{2(\infty) + 2}$ 　　　Substitute ∞ for x again.

$\dfrac{3}{\infty}$

Since the denominator is a very large number, the fraction is getting smaller. Thus the limit is zero.

0

2. $\lim\limits_{x \to 1} \dfrac{\ln x}{x-1}$ Substitute 1 for x.

$\dfrac{\ln 1}{1-1}$ The $\ln 1 = 0$

$\dfrac{0}{0}$

To find the limit, take the derivative of the numerator and denominator.

$\lim\limits_{x \to 1} \dfrac{\frac{1}{x}}{1}$ Substitute 1 for x again.

$\dfrac{\frac{1}{1}}{1}$ Simplify. The limit is one.

Practice problems:

1. $\lim\limits_{x \to \infty} \dfrac{x^2 - 3}{x}$ 2. $\lim\limits_{x \to \frac{\pi}{2}} \dfrac{\cos x}{x - \frac{\pi}{2}}$

A. Derivative of a constant--for any constant, the derivative is always zero.

B. Derivative of a variable--the derivative of a variable (i.e. x) is one.

C. Derivative of a variable raised to a power--for variable expressions with rational exponents (i.e. $3x^2$) multiply the coefficient (3) by the exponent (2) then subtract one (1) from the exponent to arrive at the derivative $\left(3x^2\right) = \left(6x\right)$

Example:

1. $y = 5x^4$ Take the derivative.

$\dfrac{dy}{dx} = (5)(4)x^{4-1}$

Multiply the coefficient by the exponent and subtract 1 from the exponent.

$\dfrac{dy}{dx} = 20x^3$ Simplify.

2. $y = \dfrac{1}{4x^3}$ Rewrite using negative exponent.

$y = \dfrac{1}{4}x^{-3}$ Take the derivative.

$\dfrac{dy}{dx} = \left(\dfrac{1}{4} \bullet {}^{-}3\right)x^{-3-1}$

$\dfrac{dy}{dx} = \dfrac{{}^{-}3}{4}x^{-4} = \dfrac{{}^{-}3}{4x^4}$ Simplify.

3. $y = 3\sqrt{x^5}$ Rewrite using $\sqrt[z]{x^n} = x^{n/z}$.

$y = 3x^{5/2}$ Take the derivative.

$\dfrac{dy}{dx} = (3)\left(\dfrac{5}{2}\right)x^{5/2-1}$

$\dfrac{dy}{dx} = \left(\dfrac{15}{2}\right)x^{3/2}$ Simplify.

$\dfrac{dy}{dx} = 7.5\sqrt{x^3} = 7.5x\sqrt{x}$

A. $\sin x$ --the derivative of the sine of x is simply the cosine of x.

B. $\cos x$ --the derivative of the cosine of x is negative one ($^{-}1$) times the sine of x.

C. $\tan x$ --the derivative of the tangent of x is the square of the secant of x.

If the object of the trig. function is an expression other than x, follow the above rules substituting the expression for x. The only additional step is to multiply the result by the derivative of the expression.

Examples:

1. $y = \pi \sin x$ Carry the coefficient(π) throughout the problem.

     $\dfrac{dy}{dx} = \pi \cos x$

2. $y = \dfrac{2}{3}\cos x$

Do not forget to multiply the coefficient by negative one when taking the derivative of a cosine function.

$\dfrac{dy}{dx} = \dfrac{^-2}{3}\sin x$

3. $y = 4\tan\left(5x^3\right)$

$\dfrac{dy}{dx} = 4\sec^2\left(5x^3\right)\left(5 \bullet 3x^{3-1}\right)$

The derivative of $\tan x$ is $\sec^2 x$.

$\dfrac{dy}{dx} = 4\sec^2\left(5x^3\right)\left(15x^2\right)$

Carry the $\left(5x^3\right)$ term throughout the problem.

$\dfrac{dy}{dx} = 4 \bullet 15x^2\sec^2\left(5x^3\right)$

Multiply $4\sec^2\left(5x^3\right)$ by the derivative of $5x^3$.

$\dfrac{dy}{dx} = 60x^2\sec^2\left(5x^3\right)$

Rearrange the terms and simplify.

$f(x) = e^x$ is an **exponential function**. The derivative of e^x is exactly the same thing→e^x. If instead of x, the exponent on e is an expression, the derivative is the same e raised to the algebraic exponent multiplied by the derivative of the algebraic expression.

If a base other than e is used, the derivative is the natural log of the base times the original exponential function times the derivative of the exponent.

Examples:

1. $y = e^x$

$\dfrac{dy}{dx} = e^x$

2. $y = e^{3x}$

$\dfrac{dy}{dx} = e^{3x} \bullet 3 = 3e^{3x}$

Multiply e^{3x} by the derivative of $3x$ which is 3.

$\dfrac{dy}{dx} = 3e^{3x}$

Rearrange the terms.

3. $y = \dfrac{5}{e^{\sin x}}$

$y = 5e^{-\sin x}$ Rewrite using negative exponents

$\dfrac{dy}{dx} = 5e^{-\sin x} \bullet \left(^-\cos x\right)$ Multiply $5e^{-\sin x}$ by the derivative of $^-\sin x$ which is $^-\cos x$.

$\dfrac{dy}{dx} = \dfrac{^-5\cos x}{e^{\sin x}}$ Use the definition of negative exponents to simplify.

4. $y = {}^-2 \bullet \ln 3^{4x}$

$\dfrac{dy}{dx} = {}^-2 \bullet (\ln 3)\left(3^{4x}\right)(4)$ The natural log of the base is ln3.

                                       The derivative of $4x$ is 4.

$\dfrac{dy}{dx} = {}^-8 \bullet 3^{4x} \ln 3$ Rearrange terms to simplify.

The most common **logarithmic function** on the Exam is the natural logarithmic function ($\ln x$). The derivative of $\ln x$ is simply $1/x$. If x is replaced by an algebraic expression, the derivative is the fraction one divided by the expression multiplied by the derivative of the expression.

For all other logarithmic functions, the derivative is 1 over the argument of the logarithm multiplied by 1 over the natural logarithm (ln) of the base multiplied by the derivative of the argument.

Examples:

1. $y = \ln x$

$\dfrac{dy}{dx} = \dfrac{1}{x}$

2. $y = 3\ln\left(x^{-2}\right)$

$\dfrac{dy}{dx} = 3 \bullet \dfrac{1}{x^{-2}} \bullet \left(^{-}2x^{-2-1}\right)$

Multiply one over the argument (x^{-2}) by the derivative of x^{-2} which is $^{-}2x^{-2-1}$.

$\dfrac{dy}{dx} = 3 \bullet x^2 \bullet \left(^{-}2x^{-3}\right)$

$\dfrac{dy}{dx} = \dfrac{^{-}6x^2}{x^3}$

Simplify using the definition of negative exponents.

$\dfrac{dy}{dx} = \dfrac{^{-}6}{x}$

Cancel common factors to simplify.

3. $y = \log_5(\tan x)$

$\dfrac{dy}{dx} = \dfrac{1}{\tan x} \bullet \dfrac{1}{\ln 5} \bullet (\sec^2 x)$

The derivative of $\tan x$ is $\sec^2 x$.

$\dfrac{dy}{dx} = \dfrac{\sec^2 x}{(\tan x)(\ln 5)}$

Implicitly defined functions are ones where both variables (usually x and y) appear in the function. All of the rules for finding the derivative still apply to both variables. The only difference is that, while the derivative of x is one (1) and typically not even mentioned, the derivative of y must be written y' or dy/dx. Work these problems just like the other derivative problems, just remember to include the extra step of multiplying by dy/dx in the result.

If the question asks for the derivative of y, given an equation with x and y on both sides, find the derivative of each side. Then solve the new equation for dy/dx just as you would an algebra problem.

Examples:

1. $\dfrac{d}{dx}\left(y^3\right) = 3y^{3-1} \bullet \dfrac{dy}{dx}$

   Recall the derivative of x^3 is $3x^{3-1}$. Follow the same rule, but also multiply by the derivative of y which

   $\dfrac{d}{dx}(y^3) = 3y^2 \dfrac{dy}{dx}$ is dy/dx.

2. $\dfrac{d}{dx}(3\ln y) = 3 \bullet \dfrac{1}{y} \bullet \dfrac{dy}{dx}$

3. $\dfrac{d}{dx}(^-2\cos y) = ^- 2(^-1\sin y)\dfrac{dy}{dx}$

   Recall the derivative of $\cos x$ is $^-\sin x$.

   $\dfrac{d}{dx}(^-2\cos y) = 2\sin y \dfrac{dy}{dx}$

4. $2y = e^{3x}$

   Solve for after taking the derivative.

   $2 \bullet \dfrac{dy}{dx} = e^{3x} \bullet 3$

   The derivative of e^{3x} is $e^{3x} \bullet 3$.

   $\dfrac{dy}{dx} = \dfrac{3}{2}e^{3x}$

   Divide both sides by 2 to solve for the derivative dy/dx.

A. Derivative of a sum--find the derivative of each term separately and add the results.

B. Derivative of a product--multiply the derivative of the first factor by the second factor and add to it the product of the first factor and the derivative of the second factor.

Remember the phrase "first times the derivative of the second plus the second times the derivative of the first."

C. Derivative of a quotient--use the rule "bottom times the derivative of the top minus the top times the derivative of the bottom all divided by the bottom squared."

Examples:

1. $y = 3x^2 + 2\ln x + 5\sqrt{x}$ $\sqrt{x} = x^{1/2}$.

$$\frac{dy}{dx} = 6x^{2-1} + 2 \bullet \frac{1}{x} + 5 \bullet \frac{1}{2}x^{1/2-1}$$

$$\frac{dy}{dx} = 6x + \frac{2}{x} + \frac{5}{2} \bullet \frac{1}{\sqrt{x}} = \frac{12x^2 + 4 + 5\sqrt{x}}{2x}$$

$$= \frac{12x^2 + 5\sqrt{x} + 4}{2x}$$

$$x^{1/2-1} = x^{-1/2} = 1/\sqrt{x}.$$

2. $y = 4e^{x^2} \bullet \sin x$

$$\frac{dy}{dx} = 4(e^{x^2} \bullet \cos x + \sin x \bullet e^{x^2} \bullet 2x)$$

The derivative of e^{x^2} is $e^{x^2} \bullet 2$.

$$\frac{dy}{dx} = 4(e^{x^2}\cos x + 2xe^{x^2}\sin x)$$

$$\frac{dy}{dx} = 4e^{x^2}\cos x + 8xe^{x^2}\sin x$$

3. $y = \dfrac{\cos x}{x}$

$$\frac{dy}{dx} = \frac{x(^-\sin x) - \cos x \bullet 1}{x^2}$$

The derivative of x is 1.
The derivative of $\cos x$ is $^-\sin x$.

$$\frac{dy}{dx} = \frac{^-x\sin x - \cos x}{x^2}$$

A **composite function** is made up of two or more separate functions such as $\sin(\ln x)$ or $x^2 e^{3x}$. To find the derivatives of these composite functions requires two steps. First identify the predominant function in the problem. For example, in $\sin(\ln x))$ the major function is the sine function. In $x^2 e^{3x}$ the major function is a product of two expressions (x^2 and e^{3x}). Once the predominant function is identified, apply the appropriate differentiation rule. Be certain to include the step of taking the derivative of every part of the functions which comprise the composite function. Use parentheses as much as possible.

Examples:

1. $y = \sin(\ln x)$

The major function is a sine function.

$$\frac{dy}{dx} = [\cos(\ln x)] \bullet \left[\frac{1}{x}\right]$$

The derivative of $\sin x$ is $\cos x$.

The derivative of $\ln x$ is $1/x$.

2. $y = x^2 \bullet e^{3x}$

The major function is a product.

$$\frac{dy}{dx} = x^2 \left(e^{3x} \bullet 3\right) + e^{3x} \bullet 2x$$

The derivative of a product is "First $\frac{dy}{dx} = 3x^2 e^{3x} + 2xe^{3x}$ times the derivative of second plus the second times the derivative of the first."

3. $y = \tan^2\left(\dfrac{\ln x}{\cos x}\right)$

This function is made of several functions. The major function is a power function.

$$\frac{dy}{dx} = \left[2\tan^{2-1}\left(\frac{\ln x}{\cos x}\right)\right]\left[\sec^2\left(\frac{\ln x}{\cos x}\right)\right]\left[\frac{d}{dx}\left(\frac{\ln x}{\cos x}\right)\right]$$

The derivative of $\tan x$ is $\sec^2 x$. Hold off one more to take the derivative of $\ln x / \cos x$.

$$\frac{dy}{dx} = \left[2\tan\left(\frac{\ln x}{\cos x}\right) \sec^2\left(\frac{\ln x}{\cos x}\right)\right]\left[\frac{(\cos x)(1/x) - \ln x(^-\sin x)}{\cos^2 x}\right]$$

$$\frac{dy}{dx} = \left[2\tan\left(\frac{\ln x}{\cos x}\right) \sec^2\left(\frac{\ln x}{\cos x}\right)\right]\left[\frac{(\cos x)(1/x) + \ln x(\sin x)}{\cos^2 x}\right]$$

The derivative of a quotient is "Bottom times the derivative of the top minus the top times the derivative of the bottom all divided by the bottom squared."

Higher order derivatives

If a question simply asks for the **derivative of a function**, the question is asking for the first derivative. To find the second derivative of a function, take the derivative of the first derivative. To find the third derivative, take the derivative of the second derivative; and so on. All of the regular derivative rules still apply.

Examples:

1. Find the second derivative $\left(\dfrac{d^2 y}{dx^2} \text{ or } y''\right)$ of the following function:

    $$y = 5x^2$$

    $$\frac{dy}{dx} = 2 \bullet 5x^{2-1} = 10 \qquad \text{Take the first derivative.}$$

    $$\frac{d^2 y}{dx^2} = 10 \qquad \text{The derivative of } 10x \text{ is } 10.$$

2. Find the third derivative (y''') of $f(x) = 4x^{3/2}$:

    $$y' = \left(4 \bullet \frac{3}{2}\right) x^{\left(\frac{3}{2}-1\right)} = 6x^{\frac{1}{2}}$$

    $$y'' = \left(6 \bullet \frac{1}{2}\right) x^{\left(\frac{1}{2}-1\right)} = 3x^{-\frac{1}{2}}$$

    $$y''' = \left[3 - \left(\frac{1}{2}\right)\right] x^{\left(-\frac{1}{2}-1\right)} = -\frac{3}{2}x^{-\frac{3}{2}}$$

Rolle's Theorem--if there are two values for x, say 2 and -3, where f(2)=f(-3), then there is some number between -3 and 2 where the derivative at that number equals zero. In other words, there is a point somewhere between $x = -3$ and $x = 2$ where the graph reaches a maximum or a minimum, like in a parabola.

Mean Value Theorem--pick two points on any curve, say $(a, f(a))$ and $(b, f(b))$. If you draw a line between these two points, the slope of it would be the change in y over the change in x or

$$slope = \frac{f(b) - f(a)}{b - a}.$$

The Mean Value Theorem says that there will be some point on the curve between $x = a$ and $x = b$ where the derivative is also equal to this slope. Set the derivative equal to this slope value and solve; doing so will produce the point where the tangent line is parallel to the line formed by connecting $(a, f(a))$ and $(b, f(b))$. Try to use the Mean Value Theorem if the problem refers to *average* rates of change.

Example:

1. The position of a particle is given by the equation $s(t) = \sin t$. What does Rolle's Theorem tell you about motion of the particle during the interval $(0, 2\pi)$?

   To use Rolle's Theorem you must first verify that $\sin t$ equals the same number for $t = 0$ and $t = 2\pi$. ($\sin 0 = 0$ and $\sin 2\pi = 0$)

   The graph of $s(t)$ shows these 2 points:

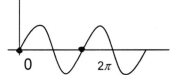

So, Rolle's Theorem states that there is at least a value between 0 and 2π so that the derivative of $s(t)$ is equal to zero.

$$\frac{ds}{dt} = \cos t$$

Set the derivative equal to zero and solve.

$$\cos(t) = 0$$
$$t = \frac{\pi}{2}, \text{ and } \frac{3\pi}{2}$$

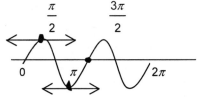

So, at $t = \frac{\pi}{2}$ and $t = \frac{3\pi}{2}$ the graph makes a turn and the tangent line is horizontal.

The derivative of a function has two basic interpretations.

    I.   Instantaneous rate of change
    II.   Slope of a tangent line at a given point

If a question asks for the rate of change of a function, take the derivative to find the equation for the rate of change. Then plug in for the variable to find the instantaneous rate of change.

The following is a list summarizing some of the more common quantities referred to in rate of change problems.

area	height	profit
decay	population growth	sales
distance	position	temperature
frequency	pressure	volume

Pick a point, say $x = {}^-3$, on the graph of a function. Draw a tangent line at that point. Find the derivative of the function and plug in $x = {}^-3$. The result will be the slope of the tangent line.

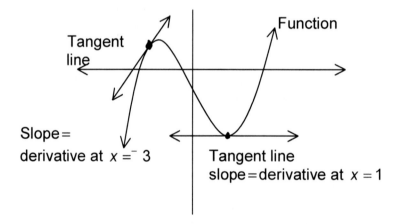

Tangent line

Function

Slope = derivative at $x = {}^-3$

Tangent line slope = derivative at $x = 1$

To find the **slope of a curve** at a point, there are two steps to follow.

    1.   Take the derivative of the function.
    2.   Plug in the value to find the slope.

If plugging into the derivative yields a value of zero, the tangent line is horizontal at that point.

If plugging into the derivative produces a fraction with zero in the denominator, the tangent line at this point has an undefined slope and is thus a vertical line.

Examples:

1. Find the slope of the tangent line for the given function at the given point.

$$y = \frac{1}{x-2} \text{ at } (3,1)$$

$$y = (x-2)^{-1} \qquad \text{Rewrite using negative exponents.}$$

$$\frac{dy}{dx} = {}^{-}1(x-2)^{-1-1}(1) \qquad \text{Use the Chain rule. The derivative of } (x-2) \text{ is 1.}$$

$$\frac{dy}{dx} = {}^{-}1(x-2)^{-2}$$

$$\left.\frac{dy}{dx}\right|_{x=3} = {}^{-}1(3-2)^{-2} \qquad \text{Evaluate at } x = 3.$$

$$\left.\frac{dy}{dx}\right|_{x=3} = {}^{-}1 \qquad \text{The slope of the tangent line is } {}^{-}1 \text{ at } x = 3.$$

2. Find the points where the tangent to the curve $f(x) = 2x^2 + 3x$ is parallel to the line $y = 11x - 5$.

$$f'(x) = 2 \bullet 2x^{2-1} + 3 \qquad \text{Take the derivative of } f(x) \text{ to get the slope of a tangent line.}$$

$$f'(x) = 4x + 3$$
$$4x + 3 = 11 \qquad \text{Set the slope expression } (4x + 3) \text{ equal to the slope of } y = 11x - 5.$$

$$x = 2 \qquad \text{Solve for the } x \text{ value of the point.}$$
$$f(2) = 2(2)^2 + 3(2) \qquad \text{The } y \text{ value is 14.}$$
$$f(2) = 14 \qquad \text{So } (2,14) \text{ is the point on } f(x) \text{ where the tangent line is parallel to } y = 11x - 5.$$

To write an equation of a tangent line at a point, two things are needed.

1. A point--the problem will usually provide a point, (x, y). If the problem only gives an x value, plug the value into the original function to get the y coordinate.

2. The slope--to find the slope, take the derivative of the original function. Then plug in the x value of the point to get the slope.

After obtaining a point and a slope, use the Point-Slope form for the equation of a line:

$$(y - y_1) = m(x - x_1)$$

where m is the slope and (x_1, y_1) is the point.

Example:

Find the equation of the tangent line to $f(x) = 2e^{x^2}$ at $x = {}^-1$.

$f({}^-1) = 2e^{({}^-1)^2}$	Plug in the x coordinate to obtain the y coordinate.
$= 2e^1$	The point is $({}^-1, 2e)$.
$f'(x) = 2e^{x^2} \bullet (2x)$	
$f'({}^-1) = 2e^{({}^-1)^2} \bullet (2 \bullet {}^-1)$	
$f'({}^-1) = 2e^1({}^-2)$	
$f'({}^-1) = {}^- 4e$	The slope at $x = {}^-1$ is ${}^-4e$.
$(y - 2e) = {}^-4e(x - {}^-1)$	Plug in the point $({}^-1, 2e)$ and the slope $m = {}^-4e$. Use the point slope form of a line.
$y = {}^- 4ex - 4e + 2e$	
$y = {}^- 4ex - 2e$	Simplify to obtain the equation for the tangent line.

A **normal line** is a line which is perpendicular to a tangent line at a given point. Perpendicular lines have slopes which are negative reciprocals of each other. To find the equation of a normal line, first get the slope of the tangent line at the point. Find the negative reciprocal of this slope. Next, use the new slope and the point on the curve, both the x_1 and y_1 coordinates, and substitute into the Point-Slope form of the equation for a line:

$$(y - y_1) = slope \bullet (x - x_1)$$

Examples:

1. Find the equation of the normal line to the tangent to the curve $y = (x^2 - 1)(x - 3)$ at $x = {}^- 2$.

$f(-2) = (({}^-2)^2 - 1)({}^-2 - 3)$ — First find the y coordinate of the point on the curve. Here, $y = {}^-15$ when $x = {}^-2$.

$f(-2) = {}^-15$

$y = x^3 - 3x^2 - x + 3$ — Before taking the derivative, multiply the expression first. The derivative of a sum is easier to find than the derivative of a product.

$y' = 3x^2 - 6x - 1$ — Take the derivative to find the slope of the tangent line.

$y'_{x={}^-2} = 3({}^-2)^2 - 6({}^-2) - 1$

$y'_{x={}^-2} = 23$

slope of normal $= \dfrac{{}^-1}{23}$ — For the slope of the normal line, take the negative reciprocal of the tangent line's slope.

$(y - {}^-15) = \dfrac{{}^-1}{23}(x - {}^- 2)$ — Plug (x_1, y_1) into the point-slope equation.

$(y + 15) = \dfrac{{}^-1}{23}(x + 2)$

$y = -\dfrac{1}{23}x - 14\dfrac{21}{23}$

$y = -\dfrac{1}{23}x + \dfrac{2}{23} - 15 = \dfrac{1}{23}x - 14\dfrac{21}{23}$

2. Find the equation of the normal line to the tangent to the curve $y = \ln(\sin x)$ at $x = \pi$.

$f(\pi) = \ln(\sin \pi)$ $\qquad$ $\sin \pi = 1$ and $\ln(1) = 0$ (recall $e^0 = 1$).

$f(\pi) = \ln(1) = 0$ $\qquad$ So $x_1 = \pi$ and $y_1 = 0$.

$y' = \dfrac{1}{\sin x} \cdot \cos x$ $\qquad$ Take the derivative to find the slope of the tangent line.

$y'_{x=\pi} = \dfrac{\cos \pi}{\sin \pi} = \dfrac{0}{1}$

Slope of normal does not exist. $\dfrac{^-1}{0}$ does not exist. So the normal line is vertical at $x = \pi$.

Finding the **rate of change** of one quantity (for example distance, volume, etc.) with respect to time it is often referred to as a rate of change problem. To find an instantaneous rate of change of a particular quantity, write a function in terms of time for that quantity; then take the derivative of the function. Substitute in the values at which the instantaneous rate of change is sought.

Functions which are in terms of more than one variable may be used to find related rates of change. These functions are often not written in terms of time. To find a related rate of change, follow these steps.

1. Write an equation which relates all the quantities referred to in the problem.
2. Take the derivative of both sides of the equation with respect to time.
   Follow the same steps as used in implicit differentiation. This means take the derivative of each part of the equation remembering to multiply each term by the derivative of the variable involved with respect to time. For example, if a term includes the variable v for volume, take the derivative of the term remembering to multiply by dv/dt for the derivative of volume with respect to time. dv/dt is the rate of change of the volume.
3. Substitute the known rates of change and quantities, and solve for the desired rate of change.

Example:

1. What is the instantaneous rate of change of the area of a circle where the radius is 3 cm?

$A(r) = \pi r^2$	Write an equation for area.
$A'(r) = 2\pi r$	Take the derivative to find the rate of change.
$A'(3) = 2\pi(3) = 6\pi$	Substitute in $r = 3$ to arrive at the instantaneous rate of change.

Taking the integral of a function and evaluating it from one x value to another provides the total **area under the curve** (i.e. between the curve and the x axis). Remember, though, that regions above the x axis have "positive" area and regions below the x axis have "negative" area. You must account for these positive and negative values when finding the area under curves. Follow these steps.

1. Determine the x values that will serve as the left and right boundaries of the region.
2. Find all x values between the boundaries that are either solutions to the function or are values which are not in the domain of the function. These numbers are the interval numbers.
3. Integrate the function.
4. Evaluate the integral once for each of the intervals using the boundary numbers.
5. If any of the intervals evaluates to a negative number, make it positive (the negative simply tells you that the region is below the x axis).
6. Add the value of each integral to arrive at the area under the curve.

Example:

Find the area under the following function on the given intervals.

$f(x) = \sin x$; $(0, 2\pi)$

$\sin x = 0$ Find any roots to f(x) on $(0, 2\pi)$.

$x = \pi$

$(0, \pi)$ $(\pi, 2\pi)$ Determine the intervals using the boundary numbers and the roots.

$\int \sin x\, dx = {}^{-}\cos x$ Integrate f(x). We can ignore the constant c because we have numbers to use to evaluate the integral.

$\left. {}^{-}\cos x \right]_{x=0}^{x=\pi} = {}^{-}\cos \pi - ({}^{-}\cos 0)$

$\left. {}^{-}\cos x \right]_{x=0}^{x=\pi} = {}^{-}(-1) + (1) = 2$

$\left. {}^{-}\cos x \right]_{x=\pi}^{x=2\pi} = {}^{-}\cos 2\pi - ({}^{-}\cos \pi)$

$\left. {}^{-}\cos x \right]_{x=\pi}^{x=2\pi} = {}^{-}1 + ({}^{-}1) = {}^{-}2$ The $^{-}2$ means that for $(\pi, 2\pi)$, the region is below the x axis, but the area is still 2.

Area $= 2 + 2 = 4$ Add the 2 integrals together to get the area.

Integration – area between two curves

Finding the area between two curves is much the same as finding the area under one curve. But instead of finding the roots of the functions, you need to find the x values which produce the same number from both functions (set the functions equal and solve). Use these numbers and the given boundaries to write the intervals.
On each interval you must pick sample values to determine which function is "on top" of the other. Find the integral of each function. For each interval, subtract the "bottom" integral from the "top" integral. Use the interval numbers to evaluate each of these differences. Add the evaluated integrals to get the total area between the curves.

Example:

Find the area of the regions bounded by the two functions on the indicated intervals.

$f(x) = x + 2$ and $g(x) = x^2$ $\begin{bmatrix} -2,3 \end{bmatrix}$ Set the functions equal and solve.

$x + 2 = x^2$
$0 = (x - 2)(x + 1)$

$x = 2$ or $x = {}^-1$ Use the solutions and the
$({}^-2, {}^-1)$ $({}^-1, 2)$ $(2, 3)$ boundary numbers to write the intervals.

$f({}^-3/2) = \left(\dfrac{{}^-3}{2} \right) + 2 = \dfrac{1}{2}$

Pick sample values on the integral and evaluate each function as that number.

$g({}^-3/2) = \left(\dfrac{{}^-3}{2} \right)^2 = \dfrac{9}{4}$ $g(x)$ is "on top" on $\begin{bmatrix} -2, {}^-1 \end{bmatrix}$.

$f(0) = 2$ $f(x)$ is "on top" on $\begin{bmatrix} -1, 2 \end{bmatrix}$.

$g(0) = 0$

$f(5/2) = \dfrac{5}{2} + 2 = \dfrac{9}{2}$ $g(x)$ is "on top" on $[2,3]$.

$g(5/2) = \left(\dfrac{5}{2} \right)^2 = \dfrac{25}{4}$

$\int f(x)dx = \int (x + 2)dx$

$\int f(x)dx = \int x dx + 2 \int dx$

$\int f(x)dx = \dfrac{1}{1+1} x^{1+1} + 2x$

$\int f(x)dx = \dfrac{1}{2} x^2 + 2x$

$\int g(x)dx = \int x^2 dx$

$\int g(x)dx = \dfrac{1}{2+1} x^{2+1} = \dfrac{1}{3} x^3$

$$\text{Area } 1 = \int g(x)dx - \int f(x)dx$$

g(x) is "on top" on $\left[^-2, ^-1\right]$.

$$\text{Area } 1 = \frac{1}{3}x^3 - \left(\frac{1}{2}x^2 + 2x\right)\Big]_{^-2}^{^-1}$$

$$\text{Area } 1 = \left[\frac{1}{3}(^-1)^3 - \left(\frac{1}{2}(^-1)^2 + 2(^-1)\right)\right] - \left[\frac{1}{3}(^-2)^3 - \left(\frac{1}{2}(^-2)^2 + 2(^-2)\right)\right]$$

$$\text{Area } 1 = \left[\frac{^-1}{3} - \left(\frac{^-3}{2}\right)\right] - \left[\frac{^-8}{3} - (^-2)\right]$$

$$\text{Area } 1 = \left(\frac{7}{6}\right) - \left(\frac{^-2}{3}\right) = \frac{11}{6}$$

$$\text{Area } 2 = \int f(x)dx - \int g(x)dx$$

f(x) is "on top" on $\left[^-1, 2\right]$.

$$\text{Area } 2 = \frac{1}{2}x^2 + 2x - \frac{1}{3}x^3\Big]_{^-1}^{2}$$

$$\text{Area } 2 = \left(\frac{1}{2}(2)^2 + 2(2) - \frac{1}{3}(2)^3\right) - \left(\frac{1}{2}(^-1)^2 + 2(^-1) - \frac{1}{3}(^-1)^3\right)$$

$$\text{Area } 2 = \left(\frac{10}{3}\right) - \left(\frac{1}{2} - 2 + \frac{1}{3}\right)$$

$$\text{Area } 2 = \frac{27}{6}$$

$$\text{Area } 3 = \int g(x)dx - \int f(x)dx$$

g(x) is "on top" on [2,3].

$$\text{Area } 3 = \frac{1}{3}x^3 - \left(\frac{1}{2}x^2 + 2x\right)\Big]_{2}^{3}$$

$$\text{Area } 3 = \left[\frac{1}{3}(3)^3 - \left(\frac{1}{2}(3^2) + 2(3)\right)\right] - \left[\frac{1}{3}(2)^3 - \left(\frac{1}{2}(2)^2 + 2(2)\right)\right]$$

$$\text{Area } 3 = \left(\frac{^-3}{2}\right) - \left(\frac{^-10}{3}\right) = \frac{11}{6}$$

$$\text{Total area} = \frac{11}{6} + \frac{27}{6} + \frac{11}{6} = \frac{49}{6} = 8\frac{1}{6}$$

SUBAREA IV. PROBABILITY, STATISTICS, AND DISCRETE MATHEMATICS

Competency 0014   Understand the principles, properties, and techniques of probability.

Dependent events occur when the probability of the second event depends on the outcome of the first event. For example, consider the two events (A) it is sunny on Saturday and (B) you go to the beach. If you intend to go to the beach on Saturday, rain or shine, then A and B may be independent. If however, you plan to go to the beach only if it is sunny, then A and B may be dependent. In this situation, the probability of event B will change depending on the outcome of event A.

Suppose you have a pair of dice, one red and one green. If you roll a three on the red die and then roll a four on the green die, we can see that these events do not depend on the other. The total probability of the two independent events can be found by multiplying the separate probabilities.

$$P(A \text{ and } B) = P(A) \times P(B)$$
$$= 1/6 \times 1/6$$
$$= 1/36$$

Many times, however, events are not independent. Suppose a jar contains 12 red marbles and 8 blue marbles. If you randomly pick a red marble, replace it and then randomly pick again, the probability of picking a red marble the second time remains the same. However, if you pick a red marble, and then pick again without replacing the first red marble, the second pick becomes dependent upon the first pick.

$$P(\text{Red and Red}) \text{ with replacement} = P(\text{Red}) \times P(\text{Red})$$
$$= 12/20 \times 12/20$$
$$= 9/25$$

$$P(\text{Red and Red}) \text{ without replacement} = P(\text{Red}) \times P(\text{Red})$$
$$= 12/20 \times 11/19$$
$$= 33/95$$

The Addition Principle of Counting states:

If A and B are events, $n(AorB) = n(A) + n(B) - n(A \cap B)$.

Example:

In how many ways can you select a black card or a Jack from an ordinary deck of playing cards?

Let B denote the set of black cards and let J denote the set of Jacks. Then,

$$n(B) = 26, n(J) = 4, n(B \cap J) = 2$$
$$= 26 + 4 - 2$$
$$= 28$$

The Addition Principle of Counting for Mutually Exclusive Events states:

If A and B are mutually exclusive events, $n(AorB) = n(A) + n(B)$.

Example:

A travel agency offers 40 possible trips: 14 to Asia, 16 to Europe and 10 to South America. In how many ways can you select a trip to Asia or Europe through this agency?

Let A denote trips to Asia and let E denote trips to Europe. Then, $A \cap E = \varnothing$ and

$$n(AorE) = 14 + 16 = 30.$$

Therefore, the number of ways you can select a trip to Asia or Europe is 30.

The Multiplication Principle of Counting for Dependent Events states:

Let A be a set of outcomes of Stage 1 and B a set of outcomes of Stage 2. Then the number of ways $n(AandB)$, that A and B can occur in a two-stage experiment is given by:

$$n(AandB) = n(A)n(B|A),$$

where $n(B|A)$ denotes the number of ways B can occur given that A has already occurred.

Example:

How many ways from an ordinary deck of 52 cards can 2 Jacks be drawn in succession if the first card is drawn but not replaced in the deck and then the second card is drawn?

This is a two-stage experiment for which we wish to compute $n(A and B)$, where A is the set of outcomes for which a Jack is obtained on the first draw and B is the set of outcomes for which a Jack is obtained on the second draw.

If the first card drawn is a Jack, then there are only three remaining Jacks left to choose from on the second draw. Thus, drawing two cards without replacement means the events A and B are dependent.

$$n(A and B) = n(A)n(B|A) = 4 \cdot 3 = 12$$

The Multiplication Principle of Counting for Independent Events states:

Let A be a set of outcomes of Stage 1 and B a set of outcomes of Stage 2. If A and B are independent events, then the number of ways $n(A and B)$, that A and B can occur in a two-stage experiment is given by:

$$n(A and B) = n(A)n(B).$$

Example:

How many six-letter code "words" can be formed if repetition of letters is not allowed?

Since these are code words, a word does not have to look like a word; for example, abcdef could be a code word. Since we must choose a first letter *and* a second letter *and* a third letter *and* a fourth letter *and* a fifth letter *and* a sixth letter, this experiment has six stages.

Since repetition is not allowed there are 26 choices for the first letter; 25 for the second; 24 for the third; 23 for the fourth; 22 for the fifth; and 21 for the sixth. Therefore, we have:

n(six-letter code words without repetition of letters)

$$= 26 \cdot 25 \cdot 24 \cdot 23 \cdot 22 \cdot 21$$

$$= 165,765,600$$

The **binomial distribution** is a sequence of probabilities with each probability corresponding to the likelihood of a particular event occurring. It is called a binomial distribution because each trial has precisely two possible outcomes. An **event** is defined as a sequence of Bernoulli trials that has within it a specific number of successes. The order of success is not important.

Note: There are two parameters to consider in a binomial distribution:

1. p = the probability of a success
2. n = the number of Bernoulli trials (i.e., the length of the sequence).

Example:

Toss a coin two times. Each toss is a Bernoulli trial as discussed above. Consider heads to be success. One event is one sequence of two coin tosses. Order does not matter.

There are two possibilities for each coin toss. Therefore, there are four (2·2) possible subevents: 00, 01, 10, 11 (where 0 = tail and 1 = head).

According to the multiplication rule, each subevent has a probability of $\frac{1}{4}\left(\frac{1}{2}\cdot\frac{1}{2}\right)$.

One subevent has zero heads, so the event of zero heads in two tosses is $p(h=0)=\frac{1}{4}$.

Two subevents have one head, so the event of one head in two tosses is $p(h=1)=\frac{2}{4}$.

One subevent has two heads, so the event of two heads in two tosses is $p(h=2)=\frac{1}{4}$.

So the binomial distribution for two tosses of a fair coin is:

$$p(h=0)=\frac{1}{4}, \quad p(h=1)=\frac{2}{4}, \quad p(h=2)=\frac{1}{4}.$$

A **normal distribution** is the distribution associated with most sets of real-world data. It is frequently called a **bell curve**. A normal distribution has a **random variable** X with mean μ and variance σ^2.

Example:
Albert's Bagel Shop's morning customer load follows a normal distribution, with **mean** (average) 50 and **standard deviation** 10. The standard deviation is the measure of the variation in the distribution. Determine the probability that the number of customers tomorrow will be less than 42.

First convert the raw score to a **z-score**. A z-score is a measure of the distance in standard deviations of a sample from the mean.

The z-score = $\dfrac{X_i = \bar{X}}{s} = \dfrac{42 - 50}{10} = \dfrac{-8}{10} = -.8$

Next, use a table to find the probability corresponding to the z-score. The table gives us .2881. Since our raw score is negative, we subtract the table value from .5.

$$.5 - .2881 = .2119$$

We can conclude that $P(x < 42) = .2119$. This means that there is about a 21% chance that there will be fewer than 42 customers tomorrow morning.

Example:
The scores on Mr. Rogers' statistics exam follow a normal distribution with mean 85 and standard deviation 5. A student is wondering what the probability is that she will score between a 90 and a 95 on her exam.

We wish to compute $P(90 < x < 95)$.
Compute the z-scores for each raw score.

$$\frac{90 - 85}{5} = \frac{5}{5} = 1 \quad \text{and} \quad \frac{95 - 85}{5} = \frac{10}{5} = 2.$$

Now we want $P(1 < z < 2)$.
Since we are looking for an occurrence between two values, we subtract:
$P(1 < z < 2) = P(z < 2) - P(z < 1)$.
We use a table to get :
$P(1 < z < 2) = .9772 - .8413 = .1359$. (Remember that since the z-scores are positive, we add .5 to each probability.)

We can then conclude that there is a 13.6% chance that the student will score between a 90 and a 95 on her exam.

Competency 0015   Understand the principles, properties, and techniques of statistics.

Percentiles divide data into 100 equal parts. A person whose score falls in the 65th percentile has outperformed 65 percent of all those who took the test. This does not mean that the score was 65 percent out of 100 nor does it mean that 65 percent of the questions answered were correct. It means that the grade was higher than 65 percent of all those who took the test.

Stanine "standard nine" scores combine the understandability of percentages with the properties of the normal curve of probability. Stanines divide the bell curve into nine sections, the largest of which stretches from the 40th to the 60th percentile and is the "Fifth Stanine" (the average of taking into account error possibilities).

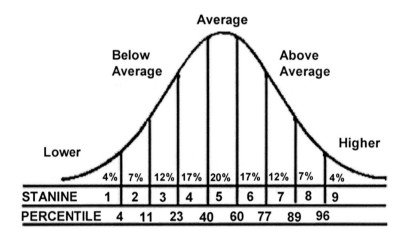

	4%	7%	12%	17%	20%	17%	12%	7%	4%
STANINE	1	2	3	4	5	6	7	8	9
PERCENTILE	4	11	23	40	60	77	89	96	

Quartiles divide the data into 4 parts. First find the median of the data set (Q2), then find the median of the upper (Q3) and lower (Q1) halves of the data set. If there are an odd number of values in the data set, include the median value in both halves when finding quartile values. For example, given the data set: {1, 4, 9, 16, 25, 36, 49, 64, 81} first find the median value, which is 25 (this is the second quartile). Since there are an odd number of values in the data set (9), we include the median in both halves. To find the quartile values, we much find the medians of: {1, 4, 9, 16, 25} and {25, 36, 49, 64, 81}. Since each of these subsets had an odd number of elements (5), we use the middle value. Thus the first quartile value is 9 and the third quartile value is 49. If the data set had an even number of elements, average the middle two values. The quartile values are always either one of the data points, or exactly half way between two data points.

Sample problem:

1. Given the following set of data, find the percentile of the score 104. [70, 72, 82, 83, 84, 87, 100, 104, 108, 109, 110, 115]

   Solution: Find the percentage of scores below 104.

   7/12 of the scores are less than 104. This is 58.333%; therefore, the score of 104 is in the 58th percentile.

2. Find the first, second and third quartile for the data listed.
   6, 7, 8, 9, 10, 12, 13, 14, 15, 16, 18, 23, 24, 25, 27, 29, 30, 33, 34, 37

Quartile 1:   The 1st Quartile is the median of the lower half of the data set, which is 11.

Quartile 2:   The median of the data set is the 2nd Quartile, which is 17.

Quartile 3:   The 3rd Quartile is the median of the upper half of the data set, which is 28.

Odds are defined as the ratio of the number of favorable outcomes to the number of unfavorable outcomes. The sum of the favorable outcomes and the unfavorable outcomes should always equal the total possible outcomes.

For example, given a bag of 12 red and 7 green marbles compute the odds of randomly selecting a red marble.

$$\text{Odds of red} = \frac{12}{19}$$

$$\text{Odds of not getting red} = \frac{7}{19}$$

In the case of flipping a coin, it is equally likely that a head or a tail will be tossed. The odds of tossing a head are 1:1. This is called even odds.

Different situations require different information. If we examine the circumstances under which an ice cream store owner may use statistics collected in the store, we find different uses for different information.

Over a 7-day period, the store owner collected data on the ice cream flavors sold. He found the mean number of scoops sold was 174 per day. The most frequently sold flavor was vanilla. This information was useful in determining how much ice cream to order in all and in what amounts for each flavor.

In the case of the ice cream store, the median and range had little business value for the owner.

Consider the set of test scores from a math class: 0, 16, 19, 65, 65, 65, 68, 69, 70, 72, 73, 73, 75, 78, 80, 85, 88, and 92. The mean is 64.06 and the median is 71. Since there are only three scores less than the mean out of the eighteen scores, the median (71) would be a more descriptive score.

Retail store owners may be most concerned with the most common dress size so they may order more of that size than any other.

Basic statistical concepts can be applied without computations. For example, inferences can be drawn from a graph or statistical data. A bar graph could display which grade level collected the most money. Student test scores would enable the teacher to determine which units need to be remediated.

To make a **bar graph** or a **pictograph**, determine the scale to be used for the graph. Then determine the length of each bar on the graph or determine the number of pictures needed to represent each item of information. Be sure to include an explanation of the scale in the legend.

Example: A class had the following grades:
4 A's, 9 B's, 8 C's, 1 D, 3 F's.
Graph these on a bar graph and a pictograph.

Pictograph

Grade	Number of Students
A	☺☺☺☺
B	☺☺☺☺☺☺☺☺☺
C	☺☺☺☺☺☺☺☺
D	☺
F	☺☺☺

Bar graph

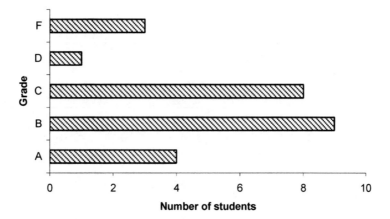

To make a **line graph**, determine appropriate scales for both the vertical and horizontal axes (based on the information to be graphed). Describe what each axis represents and mark the scale periodically on each axis. Graph the individual points of the graph and connect the points on the graph from left to right.

<u>Example:</u> Graph the following information using a line graph.

The number of National Merit finalists/school year

	90-'91	91-'92	92-'93	93-'94	94-'95	95-'96
Central	3	5	1	4	6	8
Wilson	4	2	3	2	3	2

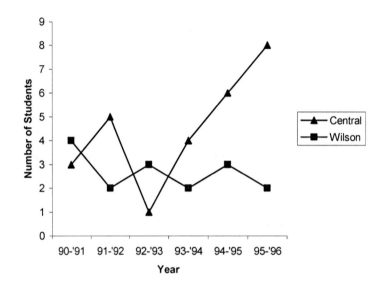

To make a **circle graph**, total all the information that is to be included on the graph. Determine the central angle to be used for each sector of the graph using the following formula:

$$\frac{\text{information}}{\text{total information}} \times 360° = \text{degrees in central} \; \square$$

Lay out the central angles to these sizes, label each section and include its percentage.

Example: Graph this information on a circle graph:

Monthly expenses:

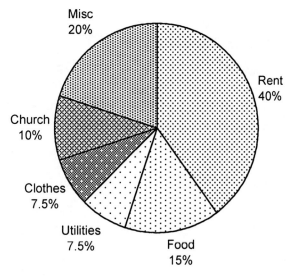

Rent,	$400
Food,	$150
Utilities	$75
Clothes	$75
Church	$100
Misc.	$200

To read a bar graph or a pictograph, read the explanation of the scale that was used in the legend. Compare the length of each bar with the dimensions on the axes and calculate the value each bar represents. On a pictograph count the number of pictures used in the chart and calculate the value of all the pictures.

To read a circle graph, find the total of the amounts represented on the entire circle graph. To determine the actual amount that each sector of the graph represents, multiply the percent in a sector times the total amount number.

To read a chart read the row and column headings on the table. Use this information to evaluate the given information in the chart.

An understanding of the definitions is important in determining the validity and uses of statistical data. All definitions and applications in this section apply to ungrouped data.

Data item: each piece of data is represented by the letter X.

Mean: the average of all data represented by the symbol X.

Range: difference between the highest and lowest value of data items.

Sum of the Squares: sum of the squares of the differences between each item and the mean.

$$Sx^2 = (X - X)^2$$

Variance: the sum of the squares quantity divided by the number of items.

(the lower case Greek letter sigma (σ) squared represents variance).

$$\frac{Sx^2}{N} = \sigma^2$$

The larger the value of the variance the larger the spread

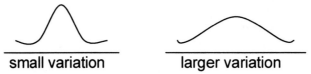

small variation   larger variation

Standard Deviation: the square root of the variance. The lower case Greek letter sigma (σ) is used to represent standard deviation.

$$\sigma = \sqrt{\sigma^2}$$

Most statistical calculators have standard deviation keys on them and should be used when asked to calculate statistical functions.   It is important to become familiar with the calculator and the location of the keys needed.

Sample Problem:

Given the ungrouped data below, calculate the mean, range, standard deviation and the variance.

| 15 | 22 | 28 | 25 | 34 | 38 |
| 18 | 25 | 30 | 33 | 19 | 23 |

Mean (X) = 25.8333333
Range: $38 - 15 = 23$
standard deviation (σ) = 6.699137

Variance (σ^2) = 48.87879

In probability, the **sample space** is a list of all possible outcomes of an experiment. For example, the sample space of tossing two coins is the set {HH, HT, TT, TH}, the sample space of rolling a six-sided die is the set {1, 2, 3, 4, 5, 6}, and the sample space of measuring the height of students in a class is the set of all real numbers {R}.

When conducting experiments with a large number of possible outcomes it is important to determine the size of the sample space. The size of the sample space can be determined by using the fundamental counting principle and the rules of combinations and permutations.

Competency 0016   Understand the principles of discrete mathematics.

The difference between **permutations and combinations** is that in permutations all possible ways of writing an arrangement of objects are given, while in a combination, a given arrangement of objects is listed only once.

Given the set {1, 2, 3, 4}, list the arrangements of two numbers that can be written as a combination and as a permutation.

Combination	Permutation
12, 13, 14, 23, 24, 34	12, 21, 13, 31, 14, 41,
	23, 32, 24, 42, 34, 43,
six ways	twelve ways

Using the formulas given below the same results can be found.

$$_nP_r = \frac{n!}{(n-r)!}$$

The notation $_nP_r$ is read "the number of permutations of n objects taken r at a time."

$$_4P_2 = \frac{4!}{(4-2)!}$$

Substitute known values.

$$_4P_2 = 12$$

Solve.

$$_nC_r = \frac{n!}{(n-r)!r!}$$

The number of combinations when r objects are selected from n objects.

$$_4C_2 = \frac{4!}{(4-2)!2!}$$

Substitute known values.

$$_4C_2 = 6$$

Solve.

Possibly the most famous sequence is the **Fibonacci sequence**. A basic Fibonacci sequence is when two numbers are added together to get the next number in the sequence. An example would be 1, 1, 2, 3, 5, 8, 13, ….

Sequences can be **finite** or **infinite**. A finite sequence is a sequence whose domain consists of the set {1, 2, 3, ... n} or the first n positive integers. An infinite sequence is a sequence whose domain consists of the set {1, 2, 3, ...}; which is in other words all positive integers.

A **recurrence relation** is an equation that defines a sequence recursively; in other words, each term of the sequence is defined as a function of the preceding terms.

A real-life application would be using a recurrence relation to determine how much your savings would be in an account at the end of a certain period of time.

For example:

You deposit $5,000 in your savings account. Your bank pays 5% interest compounded annually. How much will your account be worth at the end of 10 years?

Let V represent the amount of money in the account and V_n represent the amount of money after n years.

The amount in the account after n years equals the amount in the account after $n - 1$ years plus the interest for the nth year. This can be expressed as the recurrence relation V_0 where your initial deposit is represented by $V_0 = 5,000$.

$$V_0 = V_0$$
$$V_1 = 1.05V_0$$
$$V_2 = 1.05V_1 = (1.05)^2 V_0$$
$$V_3 = 1.05V_2 = (1.05)^3 V_0$$

......

$$V_n = (1.05)V_{n-1} = (1.05)^n V_0$$

Inserting the values into the equation, you get

$$V_{10} = (1.05)^{10}(5,000) = 8,144.$$

You determine that after investing $5,000 in an account earning 5% interest, compounded annually for 10 years, you would have $8,144.

Graphs display data so that the data can be interpreted. Graphs are often used to see trends and predict future performance.

For example, this line graph depicts the auto sales for a car dealership. The car dealership is able to see at a glance how many cars were sold in a particular month and which months tended to have the least and greatest sales. This information helps him to control his inventory, forecast his sales, and manage his staffing. He might also use the information to plan ways in which to boost sales in lagging months.

AUTO SALES

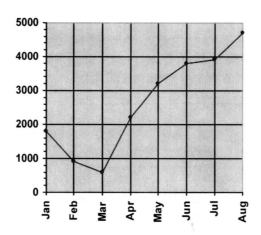

A **matrix** is a square array of numbers called its entries or elements. The dimensions of a matrix are written as the number of rows (r) by the number of columns (r × c).

$$\begin{pmatrix} 1 & 2 & 3 \\ 4 & 5 & 6 \end{pmatrix}$$ is a 2 × 3 matrix (2 rows by 3 columns)

$$\begin{pmatrix} 1 & 2 \\ 3 & 4 \\ 5 & 6 \end{pmatrix}$$ is a 3 × 2 matrix (3 rows by 2 columns)

Associated with every square matrix is a number called the determinant.

Use these formulas to calculate determinants.

2×2 $\begin{pmatrix} a & b \\ c & d \end{pmatrix} = ad - bc$

3×3
$\begin{pmatrix} a_1 & b_1 & c_1 \\ a_2 & b_2 & c_2 \\ a_3 & b_3 & c_3 \end{pmatrix} = (a_1 b_2 c_3 + b_1 c_2 a_3 + c_1 a_2 b_3) - (a_3 b_2 c_1 + b_3 c_2 a_1 + c_3 a_2 b_1)$

This is found by repeating the first two columns and then using the diagonal lines to find the value of each expression as shown below:

$\begin{pmatrix} a_1^* & b_1^\circ & c_1^\bullet \\ a_2 & b_2^* & c_2^\circ \\ a_3 & b_3 & c_3^* \end{pmatrix} \begin{matrix} a_1 & b_1 \\ a_2^\bullet & b_2 \\ a_3^\circ & b_3^\bullet \end{matrix} = (a_1 b_2 c_3 + b_1 c_2 a_3 + c_1 a_2 b_3) - (a_3 b_2 c_1 + b_3 c_2 a_1 + c_3 a_2 b_1)$

Sample Problem:

1. Find the value of the determinant:

$\begin{pmatrix} 4 & ^-8 \\ 7 & 3 \end{pmatrix} = (4)(3) - (7)(^-8)$

Cross multiply and subtract.

$12 - (^-56) = 68$

Then simplify.

Addition of matrices is accomplished by adding the corresponding elements of the two matrices. Subtraction is defined as the inverse of addition. In other words, change the sign on all the elements in the second matrix and add the two matrices.

Sample problems:

Find the sum or difference.

1.
$$\begin{pmatrix} 2 & 3 \\ {}^{-}4 & 7 \\ 8 & {}^{-}1 \end{pmatrix} + \begin{pmatrix} 8 & {}^{-}1 \\ 2 & {}^{-}1 \\ 3 & {}^{-}2 \end{pmatrix} =$$

$$\begin{pmatrix} 2+8 & 3+({}^{-}1) \\ {}^{-}4+2 & 7+({}^{-}1) \\ 8+3 & {}^{-}1+({}^{-}2) \end{pmatrix}$$
Add corresponding elements.

$$\begin{pmatrix} 10 & 2 \\ {}^{-}2 & 6 \\ 11 & {}^{-}3 \end{pmatrix}$$
Simplify.

2.
$$\begin{pmatrix} 8 & {}^{-}1 \\ 7 & 4 \end{pmatrix} - \begin{pmatrix} 3 & 6 \\ {}^{-}5 & 1 \end{pmatrix} =$$

$$\begin{pmatrix} 8 & {}^{-}1 \\ 7 & 4 \end{pmatrix} + \begin{pmatrix} {}^{-}3 & {}^{-}6 \\ 5 & {}^{-}1 \end{pmatrix} =$$
Change all of the signs in the second matrix and then add the two matrices.

$$\begin{pmatrix} 8+({}^{-}3) & {}^{-}1+({}^{-}6) \\ 7+5 & 4+({}^{-}1) \end{pmatrix} =$$
Simplify.

$$\begin{pmatrix} 5 & {}^{-}7 \\ 12 & 3 \end{pmatrix}$$

Practice problems:

1.
$$\begin{pmatrix} 8 & {}^{-}1 \\ 5 & 3 \end{pmatrix} + \begin{pmatrix} 3 & 8 \\ 6 & {}^{-}2 \end{pmatrix} =$$

2.
$$\begin{pmatrix} 3 & 7 \\ {}^{-}4 & 12 \\ 0 & {}^{-}5 \end{pmatrix} - \begin{pmatrix} 3 & 4 \\ 6 & {}^{-}1 \\ {}^{-}5 & {}^{-}5 \end{pmatrix} =$$

Scalar multiplication is the product of the scalar (the outside number) and each element inside the matrix.

Sample problem:

Given: $A = \begin{pmatrix} 4 & 0 \\ 3 & ^-1 \end{pmatrix}$ Find 2A.

$$2A = 2 \begin{pmatrix} 4 & 0 \\ 3 & ^-1 \end{pmatrix}$$

$$\begin{pmatrix} 2\times4 & 2\times0 \\ 2\times3 & 2\times^-1 \end{pmatrix}$$ Multiply each element in the matrix by the scalar.

$$\begin{pmatrix} 8 & 0 \\ 6 & ^-2 \end{pmatrix}$$ Simplify.

Practice problems:

1. $^-2 \begin{pmatrix} 2 & 0 & 1 \\ ^-1 & ^-2 & 4 \end{pmatrix}$

2. $3 \begin{pmatrix} 6 \\ 2 \\ 8 \end{pmatrix} + 4 \begin{pmatrix} 0 \\ 7 \\ 2 \end{pmatrix}$

3. $2 \begin{pmatrix} ^-6 & 8 \\ ^-2 & ^-1 \\ 0 & 3 \end{pmatrix}$

The variable in a **matrix equation** represents a matrix. When solving for the answer use the adding, subtracting and scalar multiplication properties.

Sample problem:

Solve the matrix equation for the variable X.

$$2x + \begin{pmatrix} 4 & 8 & 2 \\ 7 & 3 & 4 \end{pmatrix} = 2 \begin{pmatrix} 1 & ^-2 & 0 \\ 3 & ^-5 & 7 \end{pmatrix}$$

$$2x = 2 \begin{pmatrix} 1 & ^-2 & 0 \\ 3 & ^-5 & 7 \end{pmatrix} - \begin{pmatrix} 4 & 8 & 2 \\ 7 & 3 & 4 \end{pmatrix}$$ Subtract $\begin{pmatrix} 4 & 8 & 2 \\ 7 & 3 & 4 \end{pmatrix}$ from both sides.

$$2x = \begin{pmatrix} 2 & {}^-4 & 0 \\ 6 & {}^-10 & 14 \end{pmatrix} + \begin{pmatrix} {}^-4 & {}^-8 & {}^-2 \\ {}^-7 & {}^-3 & {}^-4 \end{pmatrix}$$

Scalar multiplication and matrix subtraction.

$$2x = \begin{pmatrix} {}^-2 & {}^-12 & {}^-2 \\ {}^-1 & {}^-13 & 10 \end{pmatrix}$$

Matrix addition.

$$x = \begin{pmatrix} {}^-1 & {}^-6 & {}^-1 \\ -\frac{1}{2} & -\frac{13}{2} & 5 \end{pmatrix}$$

Multiply both sides by $\frac{1}{2}$.

Solve for the unknown values of the elements in the matrix.

$$\begin{pmatrix} x+3 & y-2 \\ z+3 & w-4 \end{pmatrix} + \begin{pmatrix} {}^-2 & 4 \\ 2 & 5 \end{pmatrix} = \begin{pmatrix} 4 & 8 \\ 6 & 1 \end{pmatrix}$$

$$\begin{pmatrix} x+1 & y+2 \\ z+5 & w+1 \end{pmatrix} = \begin{pmatrix} 4 & 8 \\ 6 & 1 \end{pmatrix}$$

Matrix addition.

$x+1=4 \qquad y+2=8 \qquad z+5=6 \qquad w+1=1$

$x=3 \qquad\quad y=6 \qquad\quad z=1 \qquad\quad w=0$ Definition of equal matrices.

Practice problems:

1. $\quad x + \begin{pmatrix} 7 & 8 \\ 3 & {}^-1 \\ 2 & {}^-3 \end{pmatrix} = \begin{pmatrix} 0 & 8 \\ {}^-9 & {}^-4 \\ 8 & 2 \end{pmatrix}$

2. $\quad 4x - 2\begin{pmatrix} 0 & 10 \\ 6 & {}^-4 \end{pmatrix} = 3\begin{pmatrix} 4 & 9 \\ 0 & 12 \end{pmatrix}$

3. $\quad \begin{pmatrix} 7 & 3 \\ 2 & 4 \\ 3 & 7 \end{pmatrix} + \begin{pmatrix} a+2 & b+4 \\ c-3 & d+1 \\ e & f+3 \end{pmatrix} = \begin{pmatrix} 4 & 6 \\ {}^-1 & 1 \\ 3 & 0 \end{pmatrix}$

The **product of two matrices** can only be found if the number of columns in the first matrix is equal to the number of rows in the second matrix. Matrix multiplication is not necessarily commutative.

Sample problems:

1. Find the product AB if:

$$A = \begin{pmatrix} 2 & 3 & 0 \\ 1 & {}^-4 & {}^-2 \\ 0 & 1 & 1 \end{pmatrix} \qquad B = \begin{pmatrix} {}^-2 & 3 \\ 6 & {}^-1 \\ 0 & 2 \end{pmatrix}$$

$$3 \times 3 \qquad\qquad\qquad 3 \times 2$$

Note: Since the number of columns in the first matrix ($3 \times \underline{3}$) matches the number of rows ($\underline{3} \times 2$) this product is defined and can be found. The dimensions of the product will be equal to the number of rows in the first matrix ($\underline{3} \times 3$) by the number of columns in the second matrix ($3 \times \underline{2}$). The answer will be a 3×2 matrix.

$$AB = \begin{pmatrix} 2 & 3 & 0 \\ 1 & {}^-4 & {}^-2 \\ 0 & 1 & 1 \end{pmatrix} \times \begin{pmatrix} {}^-2 & 3 \\ 6 & {}^-1 \\ 0 & 2 \end{pmatrix}$$

$$\begin{pmatrix} 2(\text{-}2) + 3(6) + 0(0) \end{pmatrix}$$ Multiply 1st row of A by 1st column of B.

$$\begin{pmatrix} 14 & 2(3) + 3({}^-1) + 0(2) \end{pmatrix}$$ Multiply 1st row of A by 2nd column of B.

$$\begin{pmatrix} 14 & 3 \\ 1({}^-2) - 4(6) - 2(0) \end{pmatrix}$$ Multiply 2nd row of A by 1st column of B.

$$\begin{pmatrix} 14 & 3 \\ {}^-26 & 1(3) - 4({}^-1) - 2(2) \end{pmatrix}$$ Multiply 2nd row of A by 2nd column of B.

$$\begin{pmatrix} 14 & 3 \\ {}^-26 & 3 \\ 0({}^-2)+1(6)+1(0) & \end{pmatrix}$$ Multiply 3rd row of A by 1st column of B.

$$\begin{pmatrix} 14 & 3 \\ {}^-26 & 3 \\ 6 & 0(3)+1({}^-1)+1(2) \end{pmatrix}$$ Multiply 3rd row of A by 2nd column of B.

$$\begin{pmatrix} 14 & 3 \\ {}^-26 & 3 \\ 6 & 1 \end{pmatrix}$$

The product of BA is not defined since the number of columns in B is not equal to the number of rows in A.

Practice problems:

1. $\begin{pmatrix} 3 & 4 \\ {}^-2 & 1 \end{pmatrix}\begin{pmatrix} {}^-1 & 7 \\ {}^-3 & 1 \end{pmatrix}$

2. $\begin{pmatrix} 1 & {}^-2 \\ 3 & 4 \\ 2 & 5 \\ -1 & 6 \end{pmatrix}\begin{pmatrix} 3 & {}^-1 & {}^-4 \\ {}^-1 & 2 & 3 \end{pmatrix}$

When given the following system of equations:

$$ax + by = e$$
$$cx + dy = f$$

the matrix equation is written in the form:

$$\begin{pmatrix} a & b \\ c & d \end{pmatrix} \begin{pmatrix} x \\ y \end{pmatrix} = \begin{pmatrix} e \\ f \end{pmatrix}$$

The solution is found using the inverse of the matrix of coefficients. Inverse of matrices can be written as follows:

$$A^{-1} = \frac{1}{\text{determinant of } A} \begin{pmatrix} d & {}^-b \\ {}^-c & a \end{pmatrix}$$

Sample Problem:
1. Write the matrix equation of the system.

$$3x - 4y = 2$$
$$2x + y = 5$$

$$\begin{pmatrix} 3 & {}^-4 \\ 2 & 1 \end{pmatrix} \begin{pmatrix} x \\ y \end{pmatrix} = \begin{pmatrix} 2 \\ 5 \end{pmatrix}$$

Definition of matrix equation.

$$\begin{pmatrix} x \\ y \end{pmatrix} = \frac{1}{11} \begin{pmatrix} 1 & 4 \\ {}^-2 & 3 \end{pmatrix} \begin{pmatrix} 2 \\ 5 \end{pmatrix}$$

Multiply by the inverse of the coefficient matrix.

$$\begin{pmatrix} x \\ y \end{pmatrix} = \frac{1}{11} \begin{pmatrix} 22 \\ 11 \end{pmatrix}$$

Matrix multiplication.

$$\begin{pmatrix} x \\ y \end{pmatrix} = \begin{pmatrix} 2 \\ 1 \end{pmatrix}$$

Scalar multiplication.

The solution is (2,1).

Practice problems:

1.
$$x + 2y = 5$$
$$3x + 5y = 14$$

2.
$$^-3x + 4y - z = 3$$
$$x + 2y - 3z = 9$$
$$y - 5z = {}^-1$$

Answer Key to Practice Problems

Competency 0005, page 27

Question #1 $S_5 = 75$

Question #2 $S_n = 28$

Question #3 $S_n = -\dfrac{-31122}{15625} \approx^- 1.99$

Competency 0006, page 28

Question #2   a, b, c, f   are functions

Question #3   Domain = $^-\infty, \infty$ Range = $^-5, \infty$

Question #4   Domain = $^-\infty, \infty$ Range = $^-6, \infty$

Question #5   Domain = 1,4,7,6   Range = -2

Question #6   Domain = $x \neq 2, ^-2$

Question #7   Domain = $^-\infty, \infty$ Range = -4, 4

              Domain = $^-\infty, \infty$ Range = $2, \infty$

Question #8   Domain = $^-\infty, \infty$ Range = 5

Question #9   (3,9), (-4,16), (6,3), (1,9), (1,3)

Competency 0007, page 32

Question #1

x > 3

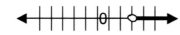

Question #2

x = 2

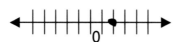

Question #3

x ≤ 6

[SA18]

Question #4

x = -4

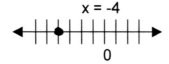

page 34

Question #1

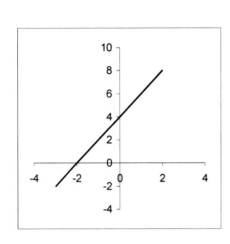

Question #2

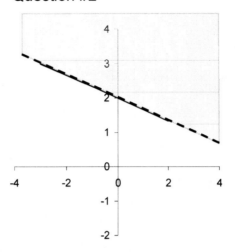

Question #3

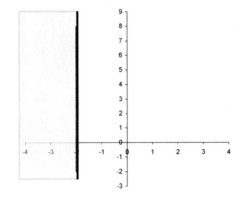

page 35

Question #1   x-intercept = -14   y-intercept = -10   slope = $-\dfrac{5}{7}$

Question #2   x-intercept = 14   y-intercept = -7   slope = $\dfrac{1}{2}$

Question #3   x-intercept = 3   y-intercept = none

Question #4   x-intercept = $\dfrac{15}{2}$ y-intercept = 3   slope = $-\dfrac{2}{5}$

page 36

Question #1 $y = \dfrac{3}{4}x + \dfrac{17}{4}$

Question #2 $x = 11$

Question #3 $y = \dfrac{3}{5}x + \dfrac{42}{5}$

Question #4 $y = 5$

Competency 0007, page 41

Question #1 $x^2 - 10x + 25$
Question #2 $25x^2 - 10x - 48$
Question #3 $x^2 - 9x - 36$

Competency 0009, page 52

Question #1 $x = 9$
Question #2 $x = 3, x = 6$
Question #3 $x = 1$

page 54

Question #1

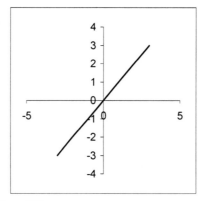

Question #2

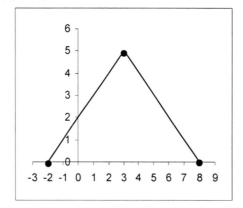

Question #3

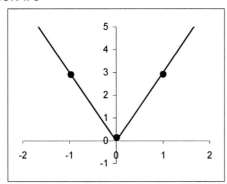

Questions #4

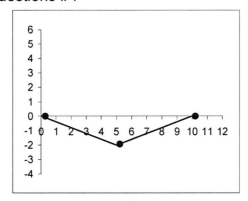

Competency 0012, page 99

Question # 1   49.34
Question # 2   1

page 100

Question #1   ∞
Question #2   -1

Competency 0016, page 136

Question #1 $\begin{pmatrix} -4 & 0 & -2 \\ 2 & 4 & -8 \end{pmatrix}$

Question #2 $\begin{pmatrix} 18 \\ 34 \\ 32 \end{pmatrix}$

Question #3 $\begin{pmatrix} -12 & 16 \\ -4 & -2 \\ 0 & 6 \end{pmatrix}$

page 137

Question #1 $\begin{pmatrix} -7 & 0 \\ -12 & -3 \\ 6 & 5 \end{pmatrix}$

Question #2 $\begin{pmatrix} 3 & \dfrac{47}{4} \\ 3 & 7 \end{pmatrix}$

Question #3 $a = -5$ $b = -1$ $c = 0$ $d = -4$ $e = 0$ $f = -10$

page 140

Question #1 $\begin{pmatrix} -15 & 25 \\ -1 & -13 \end{pmatrix}$

Question #2 $\begin{pmatrix} 5 & -5 & -10 \\ 5 & 5 & 0 \\ 1 & 8 & 7 \\ -9 & 13 & 22 \end{pmatrix}$

page 141

Question #1 $\begin{pmatrix} x \\ y \end{pmatrix} = \begin{pmatrix} 3 \\ 1 \end{pmatrix}$

Question #2 $\begin{pmatrix} x \\ y \\ z \end{pmatrix} = \begin{pmatrix} 4 \\ 4 \\ 1 \end{pmatrix}$

Sample Test

1) Given W = whole numbers
   N = natural numbers
   Z = integers
   R = rational numbers
   I = irrational numbers

   Which of the following is not true?

   A) $R \subset I$

   B) $W \subset Z$

   C) $Z \subset R$

   D) $N \subset W$

2) **Which of the following is an irrational number?**

   A) .362626262...

   B) $4\frac{1}{3}$

   C) $\sqrt{5}$

   D) $-\sqrt{16}$

3) **Which denotes a complex number?**

   A) 4.1212121212...

   B) $-\sqrt{16}$

   C) $\sqrt{127}$

   D) $\sqrt{-100}$

4) **Choose the correct statement:**

   A) Rational and irrational numbers are both proper subsets of the real numbers.

   B) The set of whole numbers is a proper subset of the set of natural numbers.

   C) The set of integers is a proper subset of the set of irrational numbers.

   D) The set of real numbers is a proper subset of the natural, whole, integers, rational, and irrational numbers.

5) **Which statement is an example of the identity axiom of addition?**

   A) $3 + -3 = 0$

   B) $3x = 3x + 0$

   C) $3 \cdot \frac{1}{3} = 1$

   D) $3 + 2x = 2x + 3$

6) **Which axiom is incorrectly applied?**

$$3x + 4 = 7$$

Step a $3x + 4 - 4 = 7 - 4$

additive equality

Step b $3x + 4 - 4 = 3$

commutative axiom of addition

Step c. $3x + 0 = 3$

additive inverse

Step d. $3x = 3$

additive identity

A) step a

B) step b

C) step c

D) step d

7) **Which of the following sets is closed under division?**

A) integers

B) rational numbers

C) natural numbers

D) whole numbers

8) **How many real numbers lie between -1 and +l ?**

A) 0

B) 1

C) 17

D) an infinite number

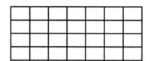

9) **The above diagram would be least appropriate for illustrating which of the following?**

A) $7 \times 4 + 3$

B) $31 \div 8$

C) 28×3

D) $31 - 3$

10) **$24 - 3 \times 7 + 2 =$**

A) 5

B) 149

C) −3

D) 189

11) Which of the following does not correctly relate an inverse operation?

A) $a - b = a + -b$

B) $a \times b = b \div a$

C) $\sqrt{a^2} = a$

D) $a \times \dfrac{1}{a} = 1$

12) Mr. Brown feeds his cat premium cat food which costs $40 per month. Approximately how much will it cost to feed her for one year?

A) $500

B) $400

C) $80

D) $4800

13) Given that n is a positive even integer, 5n + 4 will always be divisible by:

A)   4

B)   5

C)   5n

D)   2

14) Given that x, y, and z are prime numbers, which of the following is true?

A) x + y is always prime

B) xyz is always prime

C) xy is sometimes prime

D) x + y is sometimes prime

15) Find the GCF of $2^2 \cdot 3^2 \cdot 5$ and $2^2 \cdot 3 \cdot 7$.

A) $2^5 \cdot 3^3 \cdot 5 \cdot 7$

B) $2 \cdot 3 \cdot 5 \cdot 7$

C) $2^2 \cdot 3$

D) $2^3 \cdot 3^2 \cdot 5 \cdot 7$

16) Given even numbers x and y, which could be the LCM of x and y?

A) $\dfrac{xy}{2}$

B) 2xy

C) 4xy

D) xy

17) $(3.8 \times 10^{17}) \times (.5 \times 10^{-12})$

    A) 19×10^5

    B) 1.9×10^5

    C) 1.9×10^6

    D) 1.9×10^7

18) 2^{-3} is equivalent to

    A) .8

    B) -.8

    C) 125

    D) 125

19) $\dfrac{3.5 \times 10^{-10}}{0.7 \times 10^4}$

    A) 0.5×10^6

    B) 5.0×10^{-6}

    C) 5.0×10^{-14}

    D) 0.5×10^{-14}

20) Solve for x: $\dfrac{4}{x} = \dfrac{8}{3}$

    A) .66666...

    B) .6

    C) 15

    D) 1.5

21) Choose the set in which the members are <u>not</u> equivalent.

    A) 1/2, 0.5, 50%

    B) 10/5, 2.0, 200%

    C) 3/8, 0.385, 38.5%

    D) 7/10, 0.7, 70%

22) If three cups of concentrate are needed to make 2 gallons of fruit punch, how many cups are needed to make 5 gallons?

    A) 6 cups

    B) 7 cups

    C) 7.5 cups

    D) 10 cups

23) A sofa sells for $520. If the retailer makes a 30% profit, what was the wholesale price?

A) $400

B) $676

C) $490

D) $364

24) Given a spinner with the numbers one through eight, what is the probability that you will spin an even number or a number greater than four?

A) 1/4

B) 1/2

C) ¾

D) 1

25) If a horse will probably win three races out of ten, what are the odds that he will win?

A) 3:10

B) 7:10

C) 3:7

D) 7:3

26) Given a drawer with 5 black socks, 3 blue socks, and 2 red socks, what is the probability that you will draw two black socks in two draws in a dark room?

A) 2/9

B) 1/4

C) 17/18

D) 1/18

27) A sack of candy has 3 peppermints, 2 butterscotch drops and 3 cinnamon drops. One candy is drawn and replaced, then another candy is drawn: what is the probability that both will be butterscotch?

A) 1/2

B) 1/28

C) 1/4

D) 1/16

28) Find the median of the following set of data: 14 3 7 6 11 20

A) 9

B) 8.5

C) 7

D) 11

29) Corporate salaries are listed for several employees. Which would be the best measure of central tendency?

$24,000 $24,000 $26,000
$28,000 $30,000 $120,000

A) mean

B.) median

C) mode

D) no difference

30) Which statement is true about George's budget?

A) George spends the greatest portion of his income on food.

B) George spends twice as much on utilities as he does on his mortgage.

C) George spends twice as much on utilities as he does on food.

D) George spends the same amount on food and utilities as he does on mortgage.

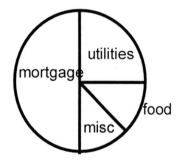

31) A student scored in the 87th percentile on a standardized test. Which would be the best interpretation of his score?

A) Only 13% of the students who took the test scored higher.

B) This student should be getting mostly B's on his report card.

C) This student performed below average on the test.

D) This is the equivalent of missing 13 questions on a 100 question exam.

32) A man's waist measures 90 cm. What is the greatest possible error for the measurement?

A) ± 1 m

B) ±8 cm

C) ±1 cm

D) ±5 mm

33) The mass of a cookie is closest to

A) 0

B) 0.5 grams

C) 15 grams

D) 1.5 grams

34) 3 km is equivalent to

A) 300 cm

B) 300 m

C) 3000 cm

D) 3000 m

35) 4 square yards is equivalent to

A) 12 square feet

B) 48 square feet

C) 36 square feet

D) 108 square feet

36) If a circle has an area of 25 cm², what is its circumference to the nearest tenth of a centimeter?

A) 78.5 cm

B) 17.7 cm

C) 8.9 cm

D) 15.7 cm

37) Find the area of the figure below.

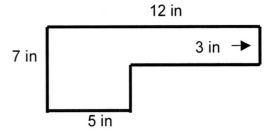

A) 56 in^2

B) 27 in^2

C) 71 in^2

D) 170 in^2

38) Find the area of the shaded region given square ABCD with side AB=10m and circle E.

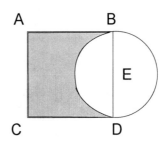

A) 178.5 m^2

B) 139.25 m^2

C) 71 m^2

D) 60.75 m^2

39) Given similar polygons with corresponding sides of lengths 9 and 15, find the perimeter of the smaller polygon if the perimeter of the larger polygon is 150 units.

A) 54

B) 135

C) 90

D) 126

40)

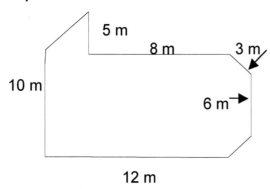

12 m

Compute the area of the polygon shown above.

A) 178 m^2

B) 154 m^2

C) 43 m^2

D) 188 m^2

41) If the radius of a right cylinder is doubled, how does its volume change?

A) no change

B) also is doubled

C) four times the original

D) pi times the original

42) Determine the volume of a sphere to the nearest cm^3 if the surface area is 113 cm^2.

A) 113 cm^3

B) 339 cm^3

C) 37.7 cm^3

D) 226 cm3

43) Compute the surface area of the prism.

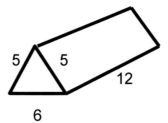

A) 204

B) 216

C) 360

D) 180

44) If the base of a regular square pyramid is tripled, how does its volume change?

A) double the original

B) triple the original

C) nine times the original

D) no change

45) How does lateral area differ from total surface area in prisms, pyramids, and cones?

A) For the lateral area, only use surfaces perpendicular to the base.

B) They are both the same.

C) The lateral area does not include the base.

D) The lateral area is always a factor of pi.

46) Given XY ≅ YZ and ∠AYX ≅ ∠AYZ. Prove ΔAYZ ≅ ΔAYX.

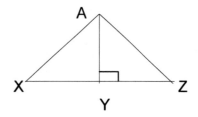

1) XY ≅ YZ

2) ∠AYX ≅ ∠AYZ

3) AY ≅ AY

4) ΔAYZ ≅ ΔAYX

Which property justifies step 3?

A) reflexive

B) symmetric

C) transitive

D) identity

47) Given $l_1 \parallel l_2$ **(parallel lines 1 & 2)**
prove $\angle b \cong \angle e$

1) $\angle b \cong \angle d$ 1) vertical angle theorem

2) $\angle d \cong \angle e$ 2) alternate interior angle theorem

3) $\angle b \cong \angle 3$ 3) symmetric axiom of equality

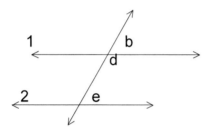

Which step is incorrectly justified?

A) step 1

B) step 2

C) step 3

D) no error

48) Simplify $\dfrac{\frac{3}{4}x^2y^{-3}}{\frac{2}{3}xy}$

A) $\frac{1}{2}xy^{-4}$

B) $\frac{1}{2}x^{-1}y^{-4}$

C) $\frac{9}{8}xy^{-4}$

D) $\frac{9}{8}xy^{-2}$

49) 7t - 4 •2t + 3t • 4 ÷ 2 =

A) 5t

B) 0

C) 31t

D) 18t

50) Solve for x:
$3x + 5 \geq 8 + 7x$

A) $x \geq -\frac{3}{4}$

B) $x \leq -\frac{3}{4}$

C) $x \geq \frac{3}{4}$

D) $x \leq \frac{3}{4}$

51) Solve for x:
$|2x +3| > 4$

A) $-\frac{7}{2} > x > \frac{1}{2}$

B) $-\frac{1}{2} > x > \frac{7}{2}$

C) $x < \frac{7}{2}$ or $x < -\frac{1}{2}$

D) $x < -\frac{7}{2}$ or $x > \frac{1}{2}$

52) $3x + 2y = 12$
$12x + 8y = 15$

A) all real numbers

B) x = 4, y = 4

C) x = 2, y = -1

D) $\varnothing$

53) $x = 3y + 7$
$7x + 5y = 23$

A) $(-1,4)$

B) $(4, -1)$

C) $(\frac{-29}{7}, \frac{-26}{7})$

D) $(10, 1)$

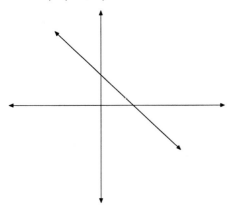

54) Which equation is represented by the above graph?

A) $x - y = 3$

B) $x - y = -3$

C) $x + y = 3$

D) $x + y = -3$

55) Graph the solution:
$|x| + 7 < 13$

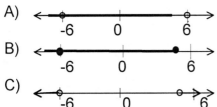

56) Three less than four times a number is five times the sum of that number and 6. Which equation could be used to solve this problem?

A) $3 - 4n = 5(n + 6)$

B) $3 - 4n + 5n = 6$

C) $4n - 3 = 5n + 6$

D) $4n - 3 = 5(n + 6)$

57) A boat travels 30 miles upstream in three hours. It makes the return trip in one and a half hours. What is the speed of the boat in still water?

A) 10 mph

B) 15 mph

C) 20 mph

D) 30 mph

58) Which set illustrates a function?

A) $\{ (0,1)\ (0,2)\ (0,3)\ (0,4) \}$

B) $\{ (3,9)\ (-3,9)\ (4,16)\ (-4,16)\}$

C) $\{ (1,2)\ (2,3)\ (3,4)\ (1,4) \}$

D) $\{ (2,4)\ (3,6)\ (4,8)\ (4,16) \}$

59) Give the domain for the function over the set of real numbers:

$$y = \frac{3x + 2}{2x - 3}$$

A) all real numbers

B) all real numbers, $x \neq 0$

C) all real numbers, $x \neq -2$ or 3

D) all real numbers, $x \neq \dfrac{\pm\sqrt{6}}{2}$

60) Factor completely:
8(x - y) + a(y - x)

A) $(8 + a)(y - x)$

B) $(8 - a)(y - x)$

C) $(a - 8)(y - x)$

D) $(a - 8)(y + x)$

61) Which of the following is a factor of $k^3 - m^3$?

A) $k^2 + m^2$

B) $k + m$

C) $k^2 - m^2$

D) $k - m$

62) Solve for x.

$$3x^2 - 2 + 4(x^2 - 3) = 0$$

A) $\{ -\sqrt{2}, \sqrt{2} \}$

B) $\{ 2, -2 \}$

C) $\{ 0, \sqrt{3}, -\sqrt{3} \}$

D) $\{ 7, -7 \}$

63) Solve: $\sqrt{75} + \sqrt{147} - \sqrt{48}$ [SA19]

A) 174

B) $12\sqrt{3}$

C) $8\sqrt{3}$

D) 74

64) The discriminant of a quadratic equation is evaluated and determined to be -3. The equation has

A) one real root

B) one complex root

C) two roots, both real

D) two roots, both complex

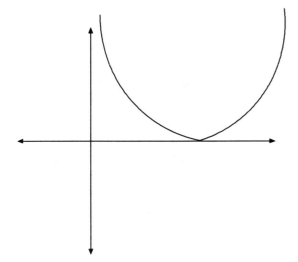

65) Which equation is graphed above?

A) $y = 4 (x + 3)^2$

B) $y = 4 (x - 3)^2$

C) $y = 3 (x - 4)^2$

D) $y = 3 (x + 4)^2$

66) If y varies inversely as x and x is 4 when y is 6, what is the constant of variation?

A) 2

B) 12

C) 3/2

D) 24

67) If y varies directly as x and x is 2 when y is 6, what is x when y is 18?

A) 3

B) 6

C) 26

D) 36

68) $\{1, 4, 7, 10, \ldots\}$.

What is the 40th term in this sequence?

A) 43

B) 121

C) 118

D) 120

69) {6,11,16,21, . .}
Find the sum of the first 20 terms in the sequence.

A) 1070

B) 1176

C) 969

D) 1069

70) Two non-coplanar lines which do not intersect are labeled

A) parallel lines

B) perpendicular lines

C) skew lines

D) alternate exterior lines

71)

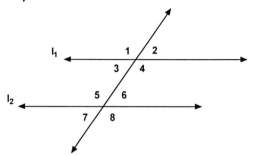

Given $l_1 \parallel l_2$
(parallel lines 1 & 2)
which of the following is true?

A) ∠1 and ∠8 are congruent and alternate interior angles

B) ∠2 and ∠3 are congruent and corresponding angles

C) ∠3 and ∠4 are adjacent and supplementary angles

D) ∠3 and ∠5 are adjacent and supplementary angles

72)

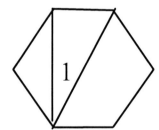

Given the regular hexagon above, determine the measure of angle ∠1.

A) 30°

B) 60°

C) 120°

D) 45°

73)

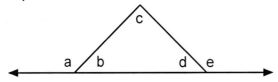

Which of the following statements is true about the number of degrees in each angle?

A) $a + b + c = 180°$

B) $a = e$

C) $b + c = e$

D) $c + d = e$

74)

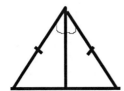

What method could be used to prove the above triangles congruent?

A) SSS

B) SAS

C) AAS

D) SSA

75)

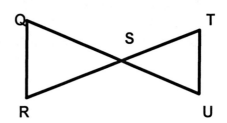

Given QS $\cong$ TS and RS $\cong$ US, prove $\triangle$QRS $\cong$ $\triangle$TUS.

I) QS $\cong$ TS	1) Given
2) RS $\cong$ US	2) Given
3) $\angle$TSU $\cong$ $\angle$QSR	3) ?
4) $\triangle$TSU $\cong$ $\triangle$QSR	4) SAS

Give the reason which justifies step 3.

A) Congruent parts of congruent triangles are congruent

B) Reflexive axiom of equality

C) Alternate interior angle Theorem

D) Vertical angle theorem

76) Given similar polygons with corresponding sides 6 and 8, what is the area of the smaller if the area of the larger is 64?

A) 48

B) 36

C) 144

D) 78

77) In similar polygons, if the perimeters are in a ratio of x:y, the sides are in a ratio of

A) x : y

B) $x^2 : y^2$

C) 2x : y

D) 1/2 x : y

78)

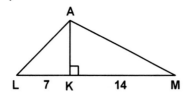

Given altitude AK with measurements as indicated, determine the length of AK.

A) 98

B) $7\sqrt{2}$

C) $\sqrt{21}$

D) $7\sqrt{3}$

79)

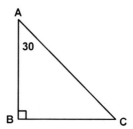

If AC = 12, determine BC.

A) 6

B) 4

C) $6\sqrt{3}$

D) $3\sqrt{6}$

80)

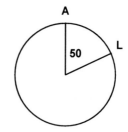

What is the measure of major arc AL ?

A) 50°

B) 25°

C) 100°

D) 310°

81)

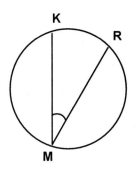

If arc KR = 70° what is the measure of ∠M?

A) 290°

B) 35°

C) 140°

D) 110°

82)

The above construction can be completed to make

A) an angle bisector

B) parallel lines

C) a perpendicular bisector

D) skew lines

83)

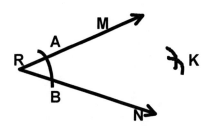

A line from R to K will form

A) an altitude of RMN

B) a perpendicular bisector of MN

C) a bisector of MRN

D) a vertical angle

84) Which is a postulate?

A) The sum of the angles in any triangle is 180°.

B) A line intersects a plane in one point.

C) Two intersecting lines from congruent vertical angles.

D) Any segment is congruent to itself

85) Which of the following can be defined?

A) point

B) ray

C) line

D) plane

86)

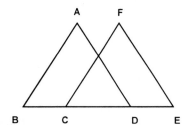

Which theorem could be used to prove △ABD ≅ △CEF, given BC ≅ DE, ∠C ≅ ∠D, and AD ≅ CF?

A) ASA

B) SAS

C) SAA

D) SSS

87)

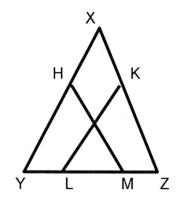

Prove △HYM ≅ △KZL, given XZ ≅ XY, ∠L ≅ ∠M and YL ≅ MZ

1) XZ ≅ XY	1) Given
2) ∠Y ≅ ∠Z	2) ?
3) ∠L ≅ ∠M	3) Given
4) YL ≅ MZ	4) Given
5) LM ≅ LM	5) ?
6) YM ≅ LZ	6) Add
7) △HYM ≅ △KZL	7) ASA

Which could be used to justify steps 2 and 5?

A) CPCTC, Identity

B) Isosceles Triangle Theorem, Identity

C) SAS, Reflexive

D) Isosceles Triangle Theorem, Reflexive

88) Find the distance between (3,7) and (-3,4).

A) 9

B) 45

C) $3\sqrt{5}$

D) $5\sqrt{3}$

89) Find the midpoint of (2,5) and (7,-4).

A) (9,-1)

B) (5,9)

C) (9/2 , -1/2)

D) (9/2, 1/2)

90) Given segment AC with B as its midpoint find the coordinates of C if A = (5,7) and B = (3, 6.5).

A) (4, 6.5)

B) (1, 6)

C) (2, 0.5)

D) (16, 1)

91)

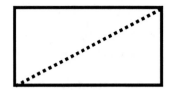

The above diagram is most likely used in deriving a formula for which of the following?

A) the area of a rectangle

B) the area of a triangle

C) the perimeter of a triangle

D) the surface area of a prism

92) A student turns in a paper with this type of error:

$$7 + 16 \div 8 \times 2 = 8$$
$$8 - 3 \times 3 + 4 = -5$$

In order to remediate this error, a teacher should:

A) review and drill basic number facts

B) emphasize the importance of using parentheses in simplifying expressions

C) emphasize the importance of working from left to right when applying the order of operations

D) do nothing; these answers are correct

93) Identify the proper sequencing of subskills when teaching graphing inequalities in two dimensions

 A) shading regions, graphing lines, graphing points, determining whether a line is solid or broken

 B) graphing points, graphing lines, determining whether a line is solid or broken, shading regions

 C) graphing points, shading regions, determining whether a line is solid or broken, graphing lines

 D) graphing lines, determining whether a line is solid or broken, graphing points, shading regions

94) Sandra has $34.00, Carl has $42.00. How much more does Carl have than Sandra?

 Which would be the best method for finding the answer?

 A) addition

 B) subtraction

 C) division

 D) both A and B are equally correct

95) Which is the least appropriate strategy to emphasize when teaching problem solving?

 A) guess and check

 B) look for key words to indicate operations such as all together-add, more than-subtract, times-multiply

 C) make a diagram

 D) solve a simpler version of the problem

96) Choose the least appropriate set of manipulatives for a six grade class.

 A) graphic calculators, compasses, rulers, conic section models

 B) two color counters, origami paper, markers, yarn

 C) balance, meter stick, colored pencils, beads

 D) paper cups, beans, tangrams, geoboards

97) According to Piaget, at which developmental level would a child be able to learn formal algebra?

A) pre-operational

B) sensory-motor

C) abstract

D) concrete operational

98) Which statement is incorrect?

A) Drill and practice is one good use for classroom computers.

B) Some computer programs can help to teach problem solving.

C) Computers are not effective unless each child in the class has his own workstation.

D) Analyzing science project data on a computer during math class is an excellent use of class time.

98) Given a,b,y, and z are real numbers and ay + b = z, Prove

$$y = \frac{z + -b}{a}$$

Statement	Reason
1) $ay + b = z$	1) Given
2) $-b$ is a real number	2) Closure
3) $(ay +b) + -b = z + -b$	3) Addition property of Identity
4) $ay + (b + -b) = z + -b$	4) Associative
5) $ay + 0 = z + -b$	5) Additive inverse
6) $ay = z + -b$	6) Addition property of identity
7) $a = \dfrac{z + -b}{y}$	7) Division

99) Which reason is incorrect for the corresponding statement?

A) step 3

B) step 4

C) step 5

D) step 6

100) Seventh grade students are working on a project using non-standard measurement. Which would not be an appropriate instrument for measuring the length of the classroom?

A) a student's foot

B) a student's arm span

C) a student's jump

D) all are appropriate

101. Change $.\overline{63}$ into a fraction in simplest form.

A) 63/100
B) 7/11
C) 6 3/10
D) 2/3

102. Which of the following sets is closed under division?

I) {½, 1, 2, 4}
II) {-1, 1}
III) {-1, 0, 1}

A) I only
B) II only
C) III only
D) I and II

103. Which of the following illustrates an inverse property?

A) a + b = a - b
B) a + b = b + a
C) a + 0 = a
D) a + (-a) =0

104. $f(x) = 3x - 2; \ f^{-1}(x) =$

A) $3x + 2$
B) $x/6$
C) $2x - 3$
D) $(x + 2)/3$

105. What would be the total cost of a suit for $295.99 and a pair of shoes for $69.95 including 6.5% sales tax?

A) $389.73
B) $398.37
C) $237.86
D) $315.23

106. A student had 60 days to appeal the results of an exam. If the results were received on March 23, what was the last day that the student could appeal?

A) May 21
B) May 22
C) May 23
D) May 24

107. Which of the following is always composite if *x* is odd, *y* is even, and both *x* and *y* are greater than or equal to 2?

A) $x + y$
B) $3x + 2y$
C) $5xy$
D) $5x + 3y$

108. Which of the following is incorrect?

A) $(x^2 y^3)^2 = x^4 y^6$
B) $m^2 (2n)^3 = 8m^2 n^3$
C) $(m^3 n^4)/(m^2 n^2) = mn^2$
D) $(x + y^2)^2 = x^2 + y^4$

109. Express .0000456 in scientific notation.

A) $4.56 x 10^{-4}$
B) $45.6 x 10^{-6}$
C) $4.56 x 10^{-6}$
D) $4.56 x 10^{-5}$

110. Compute the area of the shaded region, given a radius of 5 meters. 0 is the center.

A) 7.13 cm²
B) 7.13 m²
C) 78.5 m²
D) 19.63 m²

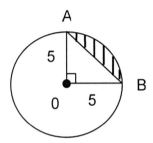

111. If the area of the base of a cone is tripled, the volume will be

A) the same as the original
B) 9 times the original
C) 3 times the original
D) 3π times the original

112. Find the area of the figure pictured below.

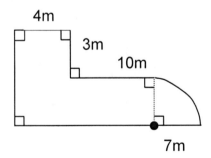

A) 136.47 m²
B) 148.48 m²
C) 293.86 m²
D) 178.47 m²

113. The mass of a Chips Ahoy cookie would be approximately equal to:

A) 1 kilogram
B) 1 gram
C) 15 grams
D) 15 milligrams

114. Compute the median for the following data set:

{12, 19, 13, 16, 17, 14}

A) 14.5
B) 15.17
C) 15
D) 16

115. Half the students in a class scored 80% on an exam, most of the rest scored 85% except for one student who scored 10%. Which would be the best measure of central tendency for the test scores?

A) mean
B) median
C) mode
D) either the median or the mode because they are equal

116. What conclusion can be drawn from the graph below?

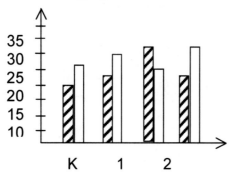

**MLK Elementary
Student Enrollment   Girls   Boys**

A) The number of students in first grade exceeds the number in second grade.
B) There are more boys than girls in the entire school.
C) There are more girls than boys in the first grade.
D) Third grade has the largest number of students.

117) State the domain of the function $f(x) = \dfrac{3x - 6}{x^2 - 25}$

A) $x \neq 2$
B) $x \neq 5, -5$
C) $x \neq 2, -2$
D) $x \neq 5$

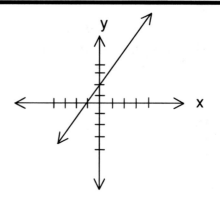

118. What is the equation of the above graph?

A) $2x + y = 2$
B) $2x - y = -2$
C) $2x - y = 2$
D) $2x + y = -2$

119. Solve for v_0 : $d = at(v_t - v_0)$

A) $v_0 = atd - v_t$
B) $v_0 = d - atv_t$
C) $v_0 = atv_t - d$
D) $v_0 = (atv_t - d) / at$

120. Which of the following is a factor of $6 + 48m^3$

A) $(1 + 2m)$
B) $(1 - 8m)$
C) $(1 + m - 2m)$
D) $(1 - m + 2m)$

121. Which graph represents the equation of $y = x^2 + 3x$?

A)

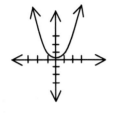

B)

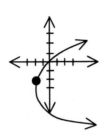

C)

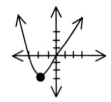

D)

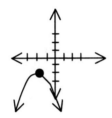

122. The volume of water flowing through a pipe varies directly with the square of the radius of the pipe. If the water flows at a rate of 80 liters per minute through a pipe with a radius of 4 cm, at what rate would water flow through a pipe with a radius of 3 cm?

A) 45 liters per minute
B) 6.67 liters per minute
C) 60 liters per minute
D) 4.5 liters per minute

123) Solve the system of equations for x, y and z.

$$3x + 2y - z = 0$$
$$2x + 5y = 8z$$
$$x + 3y + 2z = 7$$

A) $(-1, 2, 1)$
B) $(1, 2, -1)$
C) $(-3, 4, -1)$
D) $(0, 1, 2)$

124. Solve for x: $18 = 4 + |2x|$

A) $\{-11, 7\}$
B) $\{-7, 0, 7\}$
C) $\{-7, 7\}$
D) $\{-11, 11\}$

125. Which graph represents the solution set for $x^2 - 5x > -6$?

A) ⟵──○───○──⟶
     -2 0 2

B) ⟵○──────○─⟶
   -3   0

C) ⟵──○────○──⟶
     -2 0 2

D) ⟵─⟵────○○──⟶
   -3   0 2 3

126. Find the zeroes of
$$f(x) = x^3 + x^2 - 14x - 24$$

A) 4, 3, 2
B) 3, -8
C) 7, -2, -1
D) 4, -3, -2

127. Evaluate $3^{1/2}(9^{1/3})$

A) $27^{5/6}$
B) $9^{7/12}$
C) $3^{5/6}$
D) $3^{6/7}$

128. Simplify: $\sqrt{27} + \sqrt{75}$

A) $8\sqrt{3}$
B) 34
C) $34\sqrt{3}$
D) $15\sqrt{3}$

129. Simplify: $\dfrac{10}{1+3i}$

A) $-1.25(1-3i)$
B) $1.25(1+3i)$
C) $1+3i$
D) $1-3i$

130. Find the sum of the first one hundred terms in the progression.
(-6, -2, 2 . . .)

A) 19,200
B) 19,400
C) -604
D) 604

131. How many ways are there to choose a potato and two green vegetables from a choice of three potatoes and seven green vegetables?

A) 126
B) 63
C) 21
D) 252

132. What would be the seventh term of the expanded binomial $(2a+b)^8$ **?**

A) $2ab^7$
B) $41a^4b^4$
C) $112a^2b^6$
D) $16ab^7$

133. Which term most accurately describes two coplanar lines without any common points?

A) perpendicular
B) parallel
C) intersecting
D) skew

134. Determine the number of subsets of set K.
K = {4, 5, 6, 7}

A) 15
B) 16
C) 17
D) 18

135. What is the degree measure of each interior angle of a regular 10 sided polygon?

A) 18°
B) 36°
C) 144°
D) 54°

136. If a ship sails due south 6 miles, then due west 8 miles, how far was it from the starting point?

A) 100 miles
B) 10 miles
C) 14 miles
D) 48 miles

137. What is the measure of minor arc AD, given measure of arc PS is 40° and $m < K = 10°$?

A) 50°
B) 20°
C) 30°
D) 25°

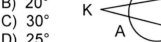

138. Choose the diagram which illustrates the construction of a perpendicular to the line at a given point on the line.

A)

B)

C)

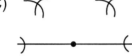

D)

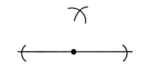

139. When you begin by assuming the conclusion of a theorem is false, then show that through a sequence of logically correct steps you contradict an accepted fact, this is known as

A) inductive reasoning
B) direct proof
C) indirect proof
D) exhaustive proof

140. Which theorem can be used to prove $\triangle BAK \cong \triangle MKA$?

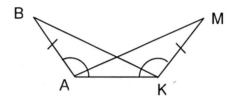

A) SSS
B) ASA
C) SAS
D) AAS

141. Given that QO⊥NP and QO=NP, quadrilateral NOPQ can most accurately be described as a

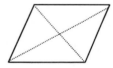

A) parallelogram
B) rectangle
C) square
D) rhombus

142. Choose the correct statement concerning the median and altitude in a triangle.

A) The median and altitude of a triangle may be the same segment.
B) The median and altitude of a triangle are always different segments.
C) The median and altitude of a right triangle are always the same segment.
D) The median and altitude of an isosceles triangle are always the same segment.

143. Which mathematician is best known for his work in developing non-Euclidean geometry?

A) Descartes
B) Riemann
C) Pascal
D) Pythagoras

144. Find the surface area of a box which is 3 feet wide, 5 feet tall, and 4 feet deep.

A) 47 sq. ft.
B) 60 sq. ft.
C) 94 sq. ft
D) 188 sq. ft.

145. Given a 30 meter x 60 meter garden with a circular fountain with a 5 meter radius, calculate the area of the portion of the garden not occupied by the fountain.

A) 1721 m²
B) 1879 m²
C) 2585 m²
D) 1015 m²

146. Determine the area of the shaded region of the trapezoid in terms of x and y.

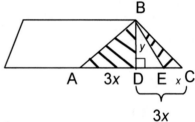

A) $4xy$
B) $2xy$
C) $3x^2y$
D) There is not enough information given.

Answer Key

1. C	38. D	75. D	112.B
2. C	39. C	76. B	113.C
3. D	40. B	77. A	114.C
4. A	41. C	78. B	115.B
5. B	42. A	79. A	116.B
6. B	43. B	80. D	117.B
7. B	44. B	81 B	118.B
8. D	45. C	82. C	119.D
9. C	46. A	83. C	120.A
10. A	47. C	84. D	121.C
11. B	48. C	85. B	122.A
12. A	49. A	86. B	123.A
13. D	50. B	87. D	124.C
14. D	51. D	88. C	125.D
15. C	52. D	89. D	126.D
16. A	53. B	90. B	127.B
17. B	54. C	91. B	128.A
18. D	55. A	92. C	129.D
19. C	56. D	93. B	130.A
20. D	57. B	94. D	131.A
21. C	58. B	95. B	132.C
22. C	59. D	96. A	133.B
23. A	60. C	97. C	134.B
24. C	61. D	98. C	135.C
25. C	62. A	99. A	136.B
26. A	63. C	100.D	137.B
27. D	64. D	101.B	138.D
28. A	65. B	102.B	139.C
29. B	66. D	103.D	140.C
30. C	67. B	104.D	141.C
31. A	68. C	105.A	142.A
32. D	69. A	106.B	143.B
33. C	70. C	107.C	144.C
34. D	71. C	108.D	145.A
35. C	72. A	109.D	146.B
36. B	73. C	110.B	
37. A	74. B	111.C	

Rationales for Sample Questions

The following statements represent one way to solve each problem and obtain a correct answer.

1) C The rational numbers are not a subset of the irrational numbers. All of the other statements are true.

2) C 5 is an irrational number. A and B can both be expressed as fractions. D can be simplified to -4, an integer and rational number.

3) D A complex number is the square root of a negative number. The complex number is defined as the square root of -1. A is rational, B and C are irrational.

4) A A proper subset is completely contained in, but not equal to, the original set.

5) B Illustrates the identity axiom of addition. A illustrates additive inverse, C illustrates the multiplicative inverse, and D illustrates the commutative axiom of addition.

6) B In simplifying from step a to step b, 3 replaced 7 - 4, therefore the correct justification would be subtraction or substitution.

7) B In order to be closed under division, when any two members of the set are divided the answer must be contained in the set. This is not true for integers, natural, or whole numbers as illustrated by the counter example 11/2 = 5.5.

8) D There are an infinite number of real numbers between any two real numbers.

9) C is inappropriate. A shows a 7x4 rectangle with 3 additional units. B is the division based on A . D shows how mental subtraction might be visualized leaving a composite difference.

10) A According to the order of operations, multiplication is performed first, then addition and subtraction from left to right.

11) B is always false. A, C, and D illustrate various properties of inverse relations.

12) A 12(40) = 480 which is closest to $500.

13) D 5n is always even. An even number added to an even number is always an even number, thus divisible by 2.

14) D x + y is sometimes prime. B and C show the products of two numbers which are always composite. x + y may be true, but not always,

15) C Choose the number of each prime factor that is in common.

16) A Although choices B, C and D are common multiples, when both numbers are even, the product can be divided by two to obtain the least common multiple.

17) B Multiply the decimals and add the exponents.

18) D Express as the fraction 1/8, then convert to a decimal.

19) C Divide the decimals and subtract the exponents.

20) D Cross multiply to obtain 12 = 8x, then divide both sides by 8.

21) C 3/8 is equivalent to .375 and 37.5%

22) C Set up the proportion 3/2 = x/5, cross multiply to obtain 15=2x, then divide both sides by 2.

23) A Let x be the wholesale price, then x + .30x = 520, 1.30x = 520. Divide both sides by 1.30.

24) C There are 8 favorable outcomes: 2,4,5,6,7,8 and 8 possibilities. Reduce 6/8 to 3/4.

25) C The odds are that he will win 3 and lose 7.

26) A In this example of conditional probability, the probability of drawing a black sock on the first draw is 5/10. It is implied in the problem that there is no replacement, therefore the probability of obtaining a black sock in the second draw is 4/9. Multiply the two probabilities and reduce to lowest terms.

27) D With replacement, the probability of obtaining a butterscotch on the first draw is 2/8 and the probability of drawing a butterscotch on the second draw is also 2/8. Multiply and reduce to lowest terms.

28) A Place the numbers in ascending order: 3 6 7 11 14 20. Find the average of the middle two numbers (7+11)12 =9

29) B The median provides the best measure of central tendency in this case, where the mode is the lowest number and the mean would be disproportionately skewed by the outlier $120,000.

30) C George spends twice as much on utilities as on food.

31) A Percentile ranking tells how the student compared to the norm or the other students taking the test. It does not correspond to the percentage answered correctly, but can indicate how the student compared to the average student tested.

32) D The greatest possible error of measurement is $\pm + 1/2$ unit, in this case .5 cm or 5 mm.

33) C A cookie is measured in grams.

34) D To change kilometers to meters, move the decimal 3 places to the right.

35) C There are 9 square feet in a square yard.

36) B Find the radius by solving $\Pi r^2 = 25$. Then substitute r=2.82 into $C = 2\Pi r$ to obtain the circumference.

37) A Divide the figure into two rectangles with a horizontal line. The area of the top rectangle is 36 in, and the bottom is 20 in.

38) D Find the area of the square $10^2 = 100$, then subtract 1/2 the area of the circle. The area of the circle is $\Pi r^2 = (3.14)(5)(5)=78.5$. Therefore the area of the shaded region is 100 - 39.25 - 60.75.

39) C The perimeters of similar polygons are directly proportional to the lengths of their sides, therefore 9/15 = x/150. Cross multiply to obtain 1350 = 15x, then divide by 15 to obtain the perimeter of the smaller polygon.

40) B Divide the figure into a triangle, a rectangle and a trapezoid. The area of the triangle is 1/2 bh = 1/2 (4)(5) = 10. The area of the rectangle is bh = 12(10) = 120. The area of the trapezoid is 1/2(b + B)h = 1/2(6 + 10)(3) = 1/2 (16)(3) = S4. Thus, the area of the figure is 10 + 120 + 24 =154.

41) C If the radius of a right ~~circular~~ cylinder is doubled, the volume is multiplied by four; because in the formula, the radius is squared. Therefore the new volume is 2 x 2 or four times the original.

42) A Solve for the radius of the sphere using $A = 4\Pi r^2$. The radius is 3. Then, find the volume using $4/3\ \Pi r^3$. Only when the radius is 3 are the volume and surface area equivalent.

43) B There are five surfaces which make up the prism. The bottom rectangle has an area 6 x 12 = 72. The sloping sides are two rectangles each with an area of 5 x 12 = 60. The height of the end triangles is determined to be 4 using the Pythagorean theorem. Therefore each triangle has area 1/2bh = 1/2(6)(4) -12. Thus, the surface area is 72 + 60 + 60 + 12 + 12 = 216.

44) B Using the general formula for a pyramid V = 1/3 bh, since the base is tripled and is not squared or cubed in the formula, the volume is also tripled.

45) C The lateral area does not include the base.

46) A The reflexive property states that every number or variable is equal to itself and every segment is congruent to itself.

47) C Step 3 can be justified by the transitive property.

48) C Simplify the complex fraction by inverting the denominator and multiplying: 3/4(3/2)=9/8, then subtract exponents to obtain the correct answer.

49) A First perform multiplication and division from left to right; 7t -8t + 6t, then add and subtract from left to right.

50) B Using additive equality, $-3 \geq 4x$. Divide both sides by 4 to obtain $-3/4 \geq x$. Carefully determine which answer choice is equivalent.

51) D The quantity within the absolute value symbols must be either > 4 or < -4. Solve the two inequalities 2x + 3 > 4 or 2x + 3 < -4

52) D Multiplying the top equation by -4 and adding results in the equation 0 = -33. Since this is a false statement, the correct choice is the null set.

53) B Substituting x in the second equation results in 7(3y + 7) + 5y = 23. Solve by distributing and grouping like terms: 26y+49 = 23, 26y = -26, y = -1 Substitute y into the first equation to obtain x.

54) C By looking at the graph, we can determine the slope to be -1 and the y-intercept to be 3. Write the slope intercept form of the line as $y = -1x + 3$. Add x to both sides to obtain $x + y = 3$, the equation in standard form.

55) A Solve by adding -7 to each side of the inequality. Since the absolute value of x is less than 6, x must be between -6 and 6. The end points are not included so the circles on the graph are hollow.

56) D Be sure to enclose the sum of the number and 6 in parentheses.

57) B Let x = the speed of the boat in still water and c = the speed of the current.

	rate	time	distance
upstream	x - c	3	30
downstream	x + c	1.5	30

Solve the system:
$$3x - 3c = 30$$
$$1.5x + 1.5c = 30$$

58) B Each number in the domain can only be matched with one number in the range. A is not a function because 0 is mapped to 4 different numbers in the range. In C, 1 is mapped to two different numbers. In D, 4 is also mapped to two different numbers.

59) D Solve the denominator for 0. These values will be excluded from the domain.
$$2x^2 - 3 = 0$$
$$2x^2 = 3$$
$$x^2 = 3/2$$
$$x = \sqrt{\tfrac{3}{2}} = \sqrt{\tfrac{3}{2}} \cdot \sqrt{\tfrac{2}{2}} = \tfrac{\pm\sqrt{6}}{2}$$

60) C Glancing first at the solution choices, factor (y - x) from each term. This leaves -8 from the first term and a from the second term: $(a - 8)(y - x)$

61) D The complete factorization for a difference of cubes is $(k - m)(k^2 + mk + m2)$.

62) A Distribute and combine like terms to obtain $7x^2 - 14 = 0$. Add 14 to both sides, then divide by 7. Since $x^2 = 2$, $x = \sqrt{2}$

63) C Simplify each radical by factoring out the perfect squares:
$$5\sqrt{3} + 7\sqrt{3} - 4\sqrt{3} = 8\sqrt{3}$$

64) D The discriminate is the number under the radical sign. Since it is negative the two roots of the equation are complex.

65) B Since the vertex of the parabola is three units to the left, we choose the solution where 3 is subtracted from x, then the quantity is squared.

66) D The constant of variation for an inverse proportion is xy.

67) B y/x-216=x/18, Solve 36=6x.

68) C

69) A

70) C

71) C The angles in A are exterior. In B, the angles are vertical. The angles in D are consecutive, not adjacent.

72) A Each interior angle of the hexagon measures 120°. The isosceles triangle on the left has angles which measure 120, 30, and 30. By alternate interior angle theorem, $\angle 1$ is also 30.

73) C In any triangle, an exterior angle is equal to the sum of the remote interior angles.

74) B Use SAS with the last side being the vertical line common to both triangles.

75) D Angles formed by intersecting lines are called vertical angles and are congruent.

76) B In similar polygons, the areas are proportional to the squares of the sides. 36/64 = x/64 $6^2:8^2$; 36:64

77) A The sides are in the same ratio.

78) B The altitude from the right angle to the hypotenuse of any right triangle is the geometric mean of the two segments which are formed. Multiply 7 x 14 and take the square root.

79) A In a 30-60- 90 right triangle, the leg opposite the 30° angle is half the length of the hypotenuse.

80) D Minor arc AC measures 50°, the same as the central angle. To determine the measure of the major arc, subtract from 360.

81) C An inscribed angle is equal to one half the measure of the intercepted arc.

82) C The points marked C and D are the intersection of the circles with centers A and B.

83) C Using a compass, point K is found to be equidistant from A and B.

84) D A postulate is an accepted property of real numbers or geometric figures which cannot be proven, A, B. and C are theorems which can be proven.

85) B The point, line, and plane are the three undefined concepts on which plane geometry is based.

86) B To obtain the final side, add CD to both BC and ED.

87) D The isosceles triangle theorem states that the base angles are congruent, and the reflexive property states that every segment is congruent to itself.

88) C Using the distance formula

$$\sqrt{[3-(-3)]^2 + (7-4)^2}$$
$$= \sqrt{36+9}$$
$$= 3\sqrt{5}$$

89) D Using the midpoint formula

x = (2 + 7)/2   y = (5 + -4)/2

90) B

91) B

92) C

93) B

94) D

95) B

96) A

97) C

98) C

99) A

100) D

101) Let N = .636363…. Then multiplying both sides of the equation by 100 or 10^2 (because there are 2 repeated numbers), we get 100N = 63.636363…

Then subtracting the two equations gives 99N = 63 or N = $\dfrac{63}{99} = \dfrac{7}{11}$.

Answer is B

102) I is not closed because $\dfrac{4}{.5} = 8$ and 8 is not in the set.

III is not closed because $\dfrac{1}{0}$ is undefined.

II is closed because $\dfrac{-1}{1} = -1, \dfrac{1}{-1} = -1, \dfrac{1}{1} = 1, \dfrac{-1}{-1} = 1$ and all the answers are in

the set. **Answer is B**

103) **Answer is D** because a + (-a) = 0 is a statement of the Additive Inverse Property of Algebra.

104) To find the inverse, $f^{-1}(x)$, of the given function, reverse the variables in the given equation, y = 3x − 2, to get x = 3y − 2. Then solve for y as follows:

x+2 = 3y, and y = $\dfrac{x+2}{3}$. **Answer is D.**

105) Before the tax, the total comes to $365.94. Then .065(365.94) = 23.79. With the tax added on, the total bill is 365.94 + 23.79 = $389.73. (Quicker way: 1.065(365.94) = 389.73.) **Answer is A**

106) Recall: 30 days in April and 31 in March. 8 days in March + 30 days in April + 22 days in May brings him to a total of 60 days on May 22. **Answer is B.**

107) A composite number is a number which is not prime. The prime number sequence begins 2,3,5,7,11,13,17,…. To determine which of the expressions is <u>always</u> composite, experiment with different values of x and y, such as x=3 and y=2, or x=5 and y=2. It turns out that 5xy will always be an even number, and therefore, composite, if y=2. **Answer is C.**

108) Using FOIL to do the expansion, we get $(x + y^2)^2 = (x + y^2)(x + y^2) = x^2 + 2xy^2 + y^4$. **Answer is D.**

109) In scientific notation, the decimal point belongs to the right of the 4, the first significant digit. To get from 4.56×10^{-5} back to 0.0000456, we would move the decimal point 5 places to the left. **Answer is D.**

110) Area of triangle AOB is .5(5)(5) = 12.5 square meters. Since $\frac{90}{360} = .25$, the area of sector AOB (pie-shaped piece) is approximately .25(π)5^2 = 19.63. Subtracting the triangle area from the sector area to get the area of segment AB, we get approximately 19.63-12.5 = 7.13 square meters. **Answer is B.**

111) The formula for the volume of a cone is $V = \frac{1}{3}Bh$, where B is the area of the circular base and h is the height. If the area of the base is tripled, the volume becomes $V = \frac{1}{3}(3B)h = Bh$, or three times the original area.
Answer is C.

112) Divide the figure into 2 rectangles and one quarter circle. The tall rectangle on the left will have dimensions 10 by 4 and area 40. The rectangle in the center will have dimensions 7 by 10 and area 70. The quarter circle will have area .25(π)7^2 = 38.48. The total area is therefore approximately 148.48. **Answer is B.**

113) Since an ordinary cookie would not weigh as much as 1 kilogram, or as little as 1 gram or 15 milligrams, the only reasonable answer is 15 grams. **Answer is C.**

114) Arrange the data in ascending order: 12,13,14,16,17,19. The median is the middle value in a list with an odd number of entries. When there are an even number of entries, the median is the mean of the two center entries. Here the average of 14 and 16 is 15. **Answer is C.**

115) In this set of data, the median (see #14) would be the most representative measure of central tendency, since the median is independent of extreme values. Because of the 10% outlier, the mean (average) would be disproportionately skewed. In this data set, it is true that the median and the mode (number which occurs most often) are the same, but the median remains the best choice because of its special properties. **Answer is B.**

116) In kindergarten, first grade, and third grade, there are more boys than girls. The number of extra girls in grade two is more than made up for by the extra boys in all the other grades put together. **Answer is B.**

117) The values of 5 and −5 must be omitted from the domain of all real numbers because if x took on either of those values, the denominator of the fraction would have a value of 0, and therefore the fraction would be undefined. **Answer is B.**

118) By observation, we see that the graph has a y-intercept of 2 and a slope of 2/1 = 2. Therefore its equation is y = mx + b = 2x + 2. Rearranging the terms gives 2x – y = -2. **Answer is B.**

119) Using the Distributive Property and other properties of equality to isolate v_0 gives d = atv$_t$ – atv$_0$, atv$_0$ = atv$_t$ – d, $v_0 = \dfrac{atv_t - d}{at}$. **Answer is D.**

120) Removing the common factor of 6 and then factoring the sum of two cubes gives $6 + 48m^3 = 6(1 + 8m^3) = 6(1 + 2m)(1^2 - 2m + (2m)^2)$. **Answer is A.**

121) B is not the graph of a function. D is the graph of a parabola where the coefficient of x^2 is negative. A appears to be the graph of $y = x^2$. To find the x-intercepts of $y = x^2 + 3x$, set y = 0 and solve for x: $0 = x^2 + 3x = x(x + 3)$ to get x = 0 or x = -3. Therefore, the graph of the function intersects the x-axis at x=0 and x=-3. **Answer is C.**

122) Set up the direct variation: $\dfrac{V}{r^2} = \dfrac{V}{r^2}$. Substituting gives $\dfrac{80}{16} = \dfrac{V}{9}$. Solving for V gives 45 liters per minute. **Answer is A.**

123) Multiplying equation 1 by 2, and equation 2 by –3, and then adding together the two resulting equations gives -11y + 22z = 0. Solving for y gives y = 2z. In the meantime, multiplying equation 3 by –2 and adding it to equation 2 gives –y – 12z = -14. Then substituting 2z for y, yields the result z = 1. Subsequently, one can easily find that y = 2, and x = -1. **Answer is A.**

124) Using the definition of absolute value, two equations are possible: 18 = 4 + 2x or 18 = 4 – 2x. Solving for x gives x = 7 or x = -7. **Answer is C.**

125) Rewriting the inequality gives $x^2 - 5x + 6 > 0$. Factoring gives (x – 2)(x – 3) > 0. The two cut-off points on the number line are now at x = 2 and x = 3. Choosing a random number in each of the three parts of the number line, we test them to see if they produce a true statement. If x = 0 or x = 4, (x-2)(x-3)>0 is true. If x = 2.5, (x-2)(x-3)>0 is false. Therefore the solution set is all numbers smaller than 2 or greater than 3. **Answer is D.**

126) Possible rational roots of the equation $0 = x^3 + x^2 - 14x - 24$ are all the positive and negative factors of 24. By substituting into the equation, we find that –2 is a root, and therefore that x+2 is a factor. By performing the long division $(x^3 + x^2 - 14x - 24)/(x+2)$, we can find that another factor of the original equation is $x^2 - x - 12$ or (x-4)(x+3). Therefore the zeros of the original function are –2, -3, and 4. **Answer is D.**

127) Getting the bases the same gives us $3^{\frac{1}{2}}3^{\frac{2}{3}}$. Adding exponents gives $3^{\frac{7}{6}}$. Then some additional manipulation of exponents produces
$$3^{\frac{7}{6}} = 3^{\frac{14}{12}} = \left(3^2\right)^{\frac{7}{12}} = 9^{\frac{7}{12}}.$$ **Answer is B.**

128) Simplifying radicals gives $\sqrt{27} + \sqrt{75} = 3\sqrt{3} + 5\sqrt{3} = 8\sqrt{3}$. **Answer is A.**

129) Multiplying numerator and denominator by the conjugate gives
$$\frac{10}{1+3i} \times \frac{1-3i}{1-3i} = \frac{10(1-3i)}{1-9i^2} = \frac{10(1-3i)}{1-9(-1)} = \frac{10(1-3i)}{10} = 1-3i.$$ **Answer is D.**

130) To find the 100th term: t_{100} = -6 + 99(4) = 390. To find the sum of the first 100 terms: $S = \frac{100}{2}(-6 + 390) = 19200$. **Answer is A.**

131) There are 3 slots to fill. There are 3 choices for the first, 7 for the second, and 6 for the third. Therefore, the total number of choices is 3(7)(6) = 126. **Answer is A.**

132) The set-up for finding the seventh term is $\frac{8(7)(6)(5)(4)(3)}{6(5)(4)(3)(2)(1)}(2a)^{8-6}b^6$ which gives 28(4a^{2}b^6) or 112a^{2}b^6. **Answer is C.**

133) By definition, parallel lines are coplanar lines without any common points. **Answer is B.**

134) A set of n objects has 2^n subsets. Therefore, here we have 2^4 = 16 subsets. These subsets include four which have only 1 element each, six which have 2 elements each, four which have 3 elements each, plus the original set, and the empty set. **Answer is B.**

135) Formula for finding the measure of each interior angle of a regular polygon with n sides is $\frac{(n-2)180}{n}$. For n=10, we get $\frac{8(180)}{10} = 144$. **Answer is C.**

136) Draw a right triangle with legs of 6 and 8. Find the hypotenuse using the Pythagorean Theorem. $6^2 + 8^2 = c^2$. Therefore, c = 10 miles. **Answer is B.**

137) The formula relating the measure of angle K and the two arcs it intercepts is $m\angle K = \frac{1}{2}(mPS - mAD)$. Substituting the known values, we get $10 = \frac{1}{2}(40 - mAD)$. Solving for mAD gives an answer of 20 degrees. **Answer is B.**

138) Given a point on a line, place the compass point there and draw two arcs intersecting the line in two points, one on either side of the given point. Then using any radius larger than half the new segment produced, and with the pointer at each end of the new segment, draw arcs which intersect above the line. Connect this new point with the given point. **Answer is D.**

139) By definition this describes the procedure of an indirect proof. **Answer is C.**

140) Since side AK is common to both triangles, the triangles can be proved congruent by using the Side-Angle-Side Postulate. **Answer is C.**

141) In an ordinary parallelogram, the diagonals are not perpendicular or equal in length. In a rectangle, the diagonals are not necessarily perpendicular. In a rhombus, the diagonals are not equal in length. In a square, the diagonals are both perpendicular and congruent. **Answer is C.**

142) The most one can say with certainty is that the median (segment drawn to the midpoint of the opposite side) and the altitude (segment drawn perpendicular to the opposite side) of a triangle <u>may</u> coincide, but they more often do not. In an isosceles triangle, the median and the altitude to the <u>base</u> are the same segment. **Answer is A.**

143) In the mid-nineteenth century, Reimann and other mathematicians developed elliptic geometry. **Answer is B.**

144) Let's assume the base of the rectangular solid (box) is 3 by 4, and the height is 5. Then the surface area of the top and bottom together is 2(12) = 24. The sum of the areas of the front and back are 2(15) = 30, while the sum of the areas of the sides are 2(20)=40. The total surface area is therefore 94 square feet. **Answer is C.**

145) Find the area of the garden and then subtract the area of the fountain: $30(60) - \pi(5)^2$ or approximately 1721 square meters. **Answer is A.**

146) To find the area of the shaded region, find the area of triangle ABC and then subtract the area of triangle DBE. The area of triangle ABC is .5(6x)(y) = 3xy. The area of triangle DBE is .5(2x)(y) = xy. The difference is 2xy. **Answer is B.**

XAMonline, INC. 21 Orient Ave. Melrose, MA 02176

Toll Free number 800-509-4128

TO ORDER Fax 781-662-9268 OR www.XAMonline.com

CERTIFICATION EXAMINATION FOR OKLAHOMA EDUCATORS   - CEOE - 2007

PO#   Store/School:

Address 1:

Address 2 (Ship to other):

City, State Zip

Credit card number_____-_____-_____-_____   expiration_____

EMAIL _____

PHONE   **FAX**

13# ISBN 2007	TITLE	Qty	Retail	Total
978-1-58197-646-5	CEOE OSAT Advanced Mathematics Field 11			
978-1-58197-775-2	CEOE OSAT Art Sample Test Field 02			
978-1-58197-780-6	CEOE OSAT Biological Sciences Field 10			
978-1-58197-776-9	CEOE OSAT Chemistry Field 04			
978-1-58197-778-3	CEOE OSAT Earth Science Field 08			
978-1-58197-794-3	CEOE OSAT Elementary Education Fields 50-51			
978-1-58197-795-0	CEOE OSAT Elementary Education Fields 50-51 Sample Questions			
978-1-58197-777-6	CEOE OSAT English Field 07			
978-1-58197-779-0	CEOE OSAT Family and Consumer Sciences Field 09			
978-1-58197-786-8	CEOE OSAT French Sample Test Field 20			
978-1-58197-798-1	CEOE OGET Oklahoma General Education Test 074			
978-1-58197-792-9	CEOE OSAT Library-Media Specialist Field 38			
978-1-58197-787-5	CEOE OSAT Middle Level English Field 24			
978-1-58197-789-9	CEOE OSAT Middle Level Science Field 26			
978-1-58197-790-5	CEOE OSAT Middle Level Social Studies Field 27			
978-1-58197-647-2	CEOE OSAT Middle Level-Intermediate Mathematics Field 25			
978-1-58197-791-2	CEOE OSAT Mild Moderate Disabilities Field 29			
978-1-58197-782-0	CEOE OSAT Physical Education-Health-Safety Field 12			
978-1-58197-783-7	CEOE OSAT Physics Sample Test Field 14			
978-1-58197-793-6	CEOE OSAT Principal Common Core Field 44			
978-1-58197-796-7	CEOE OPTE Oklahoma Professional Teaching Examination Fields 75-76			
978-1-58197-784-4	CEOE OSAT Reading Specialist Field 15			
978-1-58197-785-1	CEOE OSAT Spanish Field 19			
978-1-58197-797-4	CEOE OSAT U.S. & World History Field 17			
			SUBTOTAL	
	FOR PRODUCT PRICES GO TO WWW.XAMONLINE.COM		**Ship**	$8.25
			TOTAL	

CPSIA information can be obtained at www.ICGtesting.com
Printed in the USA
BVOW04s0428260215

389333BV00005B/205/P